The Library of Scandinavian Literature

WORLD HISTORICAL PLAYS

WORLD HISTORICAL PLAYS

AUGUST STRINDBERG

TRANSLATED FROM THE SWEDISH BY
ARVID PAULSON

INTRODUCTION BY
GUNNAR OLLÉN

SAN DIEGO PUBLIC LIBRARY

TWAYNE PUBLISHERS, INC., NEW YORK
&
THE AMERICAN-SCANDINAVIAN FOUNDATION

The Library of Scandinavian Literature
Erik J. Friis, *General Editor*

Volume 6

World Historical Plays by August Strindberg

The Nightingale of Wittenberg (Martin Luther)
Copyright © 1969 by Arvid Paulson

Through Deserts to Ancestral Lands (Moses)
Copyright © 1960 by Arvid Paulson

Hellas (Socrates) Copyright © 1960 by Arvid Paulson

The Lamb and the Beast (Christ)
Copyright © 1960 by Arvid Paulson

Copyright © 1970 by Twayne Publishers, Inc.
Library of Congress catalogue card number: 75-120537

THESE TRANSLATIONS ARE DEDICATED TO
GUNNAR JARRING

Contents

Introduction

When August Strindberg was in the clutches of his Inferno crisis in Paris, Austria, and the south of Sweden during the middle of the 1890's, his literary production was practically at a standstill. But in 1898 his dramatic creativity blossomed anew. His creative energy was like a dammed-up river breaking down all barriers. Within four years he had written a score of dramas, among which were such masterly works as *The Dance of Death, A Dream Play, Easter,* and *To Damascus.*

Première followed première in Stockholm and in Germany. However, this enormous productivity was more than the theaters could absorb. For certain of these plays the technical resources of that time were insufficient and scenically undeveloped so that full justice could not be given to the imaginative Strindbergian leaps of fantasy.

Strindberg became conscious of the necessity of attempting and pursuing other paths and methods in his production.

He wrote some lyrical and prose works; and after that he turned to history, not to the history of Sweden, with which he had occupied himself earlier, but to the history of other nations. Germany's past interested him in particular. It was in Germany that his dramas had found even greater appreciation than in his native Sweden. In 1902 *Crimes and Crimes* had had a magnificent reception in Berlin; in Schwerin *Erik XIV* was being played, and *Easter* was having an extended run in Munich. If he were now to take on another historical subject, he felt that it ought to deal with a phase of German history in order that it may have a strong appeal to theatergoers in that country. On November 25, 1902, he wrote to his German admirer and translator Emil

Schering asking that he send him at the earliest moment a popular book about Faust and also the writings of Hans Sachs. On December 8 of the same year Strindberg denied a newspaper rumor to the effect that he was engaged in work on a drama about Martin Luther, admitting, however, that the thought of writing such a drama had long been tempting him.

Already before this time he had mentioned in a letter to Schering that he had "perused the history of the world from beginning to end" as a diversion. He had previously likened history to a robber novel, but later found that history was a product of a conscious will—the will of God. In the spring of 1903, his religiously inspired view of history was exposed in a series of articles published in the Stockholm newspaper *Svenska Dagbladet* under the title "The Mysticism of World History." In it he alluded frequently to Luther but spoke of him without any special respect. Thus "Luther was a man of division, who began with denials and ended up with assertions and declarations; and to agree with him in all his self-contradictions is well-nigh intolerable. . . . A man of Providence, a man from the rank and file of the people who blindly plunges ahead without being conscious of the Lord's intentions, a formidable instrument, a symbol of contradictions and a rock of offence, a human being full of arrogance and humility, clear of mind but unclear of purpose—this was Luther." This gruff, stern opinion of Luther was the development of views from Strindberg's Nietzsche period around 1890. The German philosopher had repeatedly ridiculed Luther as a "peasant" and as a "northern barbarian intellectual."

Nonetheless, there was much in the German reformer which profoundly impressed Strindberg. There were even moments when he felt that they were soul mates. Luther's severe childhood years reminded Strindberg of his own. Like Strindberg, Luther had been beaten and abused severely, sometimes unjustly, by his father who was of a stern, rough nature. Strindberg also understood Luther's longing for the peace of a monastic retreat and why Luther rebelled against rigorous rules, especially those pertaining to strict, unquestioning obedience. Strindberg's own brief experience of twenty-four hours in the Belgian monastery Maredsous, which he visited in 1898, helped him to understand Luther's objections.

But what most of all made Strindberg feel a spiritual affinity for Luther was his great loneliness and the fact that he so courageously defied prevalent opinions and the men in power. When Luther had been released from his monastic vows and had broken with his friends, Strindberg has Luther speak these words: "Alone! . . . So much the better! Almighty, living God! Now You and I stand alone!" These same words Strindberg could have spoken about himself when he at long last penned his drama between August 21 and September 5, 1903.

In March of that year Strindberg's third marriage—to the distinguished actress Harriet Bosse—had been stormier than ever. She had consulted an attorney about obtaining a divorce after a marriage of less than two years. The relationship had been barely resumed, however, before it broke up again during a visit to the Stockholm skerries in the beginning of July. On August 1, Strindberg confides to his diary (*The Occult Diary*, published 1963): "Eradicated from the apartment all the little knick-knacks that had belonged to Harriet." She and their little daughter Anne-Marie rented a flat elsewhere. It was not until the Luther drama had been completed that the couple resumed contact with each other, although merely to a limited extent.

In this drama, ironically named *The Nightingale of Wittenberg*, one can watch "Germany's biggest blusterer" throughout a broadly built up historical cavalcade, beginning with the controversies in the parental home, progress-

ing through the discontent and unhappiness from his con-
finement in the Augustinian monastery at Erfurt up to the
nailing onto the church portal at Wittenberg of the ninety-
five theses protesting the sale of pardons and releases from
Purgatory, the critical days in Worms, and ending with his
stay in the castle of Wartburg.

In spite of the length of the drama, one never seems to
obtain a clear perspective of the leading characters. Strindberg bestows on his hero a critically mixed admiration but
never penetrates to the core of his personality. The dramatic
picture is chopped up into a number of minor scenes. Here
and there the dramatist amuses himself by offering a critical
revue of culture, in which a number of universally famed
characters participate: Erasmus, Ulrich von Hutten—who
stubbornly dwells upon his syphilis—, Hans Sachs, Lucas
Cranach, Philip Melanchthon and others. Doctor Johannes
Faust is also involved in the play.

Strindberg himself held the opinion that this drama was
superior to *Gustaf Vasa* and *Master Olof*, his dramas of
Swedish history. "It is the strongest and most youthful that
I have written! No doubts as in *Master Olof*, no scruples, no
women around your neck, no parents standing in the way,
no compromising with friends," he wrote to his German
translator Emil Schering. And in a letter to the publisher
Hugo Geber he called it "my best, most beautiful and possibly my last drama" (May 17, 1904). He had at that time
not yet written his chamber plays (*The Pelican, Storm-
clouds, The Ghost Sonata, The Burned Premise*, and *The
Black Glove*), nor *The Great Highway* and other important
plays.

In the history of the theater Strindberg's high appreciation of his play has not been proven to have been justified.
The superficial delineation of the characters, the dizzy
scurrying through the fourteen scenes of the play, the
abundance of minor characters and the lack of tension have

made the play difficult to stage and to act.

Die Nachtigall von Wittenberg, or *Luther,* was given its original performance at the Deutches Künstlertheater in Berlin on December 5, 1914, with Friedrich Kayssler in the leading role. It was produced in Hamburg in 1915 and 1917, and in Vienna in 1918. The play had its American première in German at the Irving Place Theatre in 1917, staged by Rudolf Christians, the father of Mady Christians. When the play had its première in Sweden (at The Swedish Theater) on January 26, 1917, the critical reception was far from encouraging. It met with a similar fate when it was produced in Gothenburg in 1927. Since then the somewhat unmelodious *Nightingale* has not opened up its nib.

Strindberg was not content with dramatizing only this portion of world history. No sooner had he in the early part of September, 1903, completed *The Nightingale of Wittenberg* than he seems to have set to work upon the next drama in this cycle.

His intention was to proceed in his task methodically and so put into effect his previous plans. Already in 1884, in a letter to Karl Otto Bonnier, the Stockholm publisher, he had proposed that Bonnier subsidize him for studies abroad in connection with a trilogy "dealing exclusively with world history: India, Egypt, Palestine, Greece, Rome, the Middle Ages, the Reformation, and ending with the French Revolution." This plan of his had come to naught as had a similar idea that he in 1889 had unfolded to the distinguished actor-producer August Lindberg: "A pilgrimage through the history of the world—Hellas, Golgotha, Rome, the Middle Ages, etc."

He now decided to realize his intentions by writing a giant cycle of dramas, not less than three, each one in five acts; one of these was to be *The Nightingale of Wittenberg.*

But he had good cause to feel dubious as to whether the

subjects would not have greater general appeal if treated in the form of a novel, or if written as historical tales. Nevertheless, he finished three short plays with Moses, Socrates, and Christ as chief protagonists, in this order. After that he tired of the task.

The first one of these dramas in the world historical cycle, *Through Deserts to Ancestral Lands* (*Moses*), is a simply arranged paraphrasing of the Bible stories of Moses' leading the Jews out of Egypt through the deserts into the land of Canaan. The fruits of Strindberg's reading are plainly visible and the archaic dialogue dangles, somewhat untouched by the breath of inspiration.

Moses has had a production in Germany, where it was given at the Civic Theater in Hanover during the autumn of 1922.

The second drama in the world historical series, *Hellas*, or *Socrates*, was begun, according to the author's *Occult Diary*, in the middle of October, 1903, and was seemingly completed a week or two later. Much as in his early poetic drama *Hermione*, which he wrote in 1870 at the age of twenty-one, it describes Hellas in its state of dissolution. There is in this drama no definable action. Through the nineteen scenes of the play one hears Socrates, Pericles, Protagoras, Plato, Phidias, Euripides, and other renowned men discussing politics, their gods, and the woman question. One is aware that the author in this play is somewhat more engaged with the subject than in the *Moses* play. He felt warmly for Euripides—who might be said to have been a Strindberg of antiquity—but he had nothing but scorn and disdain for the jester Aristophanes. In fact, Strindberg abhorred authors of this type generally, just as he disliked those who made jest of or caricatured him.

But Socrates was the man to whom Strindberg felt closest. As far back as 1887 Strindberg—in a letter to the author

Axel Lundegård—had written: "Have been seized with an ardent sympathy for Socrates and am today dreaming of writing a play about him in contemporary form and language."

Socrates is in this drama made to prepare the ground for Strindberg's theme by virtue of his skepticism toward the pagan gods: classical antiquity is in the throes of getting ready to accept the Unknown God, the only God—the God who saved Moses and the children of Israel from the Egyptian captivity. As a link in the drama the figure of Cartaphilus, the shoemaker of Jerusalem, the wandering Jew— so dear to Strindberg—runs through it.

Socrates also evoked Strindberg's sympathy by his critical attitude toward woman and marriage. The world-famous sage and philosopher is made to deliver a great many venomous Strindbergian remarks against his Xanthippe before he empties the poisoned draft in the final scene. He then says: "Think of it, I slave for my worst enemy and feed her and house her—and she carries on a war against me—for which I have to pay the cost. . . ." But Socrates pays tribute to the bohemian Aspasia, the maiden who inspires the men to "give birth to thoughts." The model for Aspasia, the young Norwegian woman Dagny Juel, to whom Strindberg and the Berlin coterie of bohemian artists, poets, and other literary figures and musicians paid court in the spring of 1893, had died in the summer of 1903; and in this drama Strindberg pays her homage posthumously.

The words of leave-taking that Socrates addresses to his favorite disciple, Plato, present a quite sensitive expression of Strindberg's own credo in the fall of 1903: "You shall teach humanity to look with sober restraint upon the things we see with our senses—to look up to the unseen with reverence—to pay homage to beauty—to cultivate virtue and to hope for our deliverance—through labor, sacrifices, and the performance of our duties. . . ."

The world première of this play was given in the fall of 1922 at the Civic Theater in Hanover, when both *Socrates* and *Moses* appeared on the same bill. In Sweden *Socrates* was first presented in Stockholm in 1942, at the Dramatiker-studio. It turned out to be an interesting performance, not least because of the successful pictorial background, the Acropolis in dazzling white, set against a blue cyclorama.

The third one in the cycle of world historical dramas, *The Lamb and the Beast*, or *Christ*, was commenced by Strind-berg, according to *The Occult Diary*, in the vicinity of Octo-ber 19, 1903, and on November 5 of that year he had com-pleted it. He first titled it *The Messiah and the Anti-Messiah*. With this play Strindberg brought to an end his plan from his young manhood years to write a drama about Jesus of Nazareth.

The coloring of this play is more striking, more extrava-gant, than in the two preceding ones. The drama begins with the birth of Christ the Saviour in Bethlehem, and his death on the cross at Golgotha. Christ is merely spoken of, and Golgotha is effectively symbolized by the shadows of three crosses falling against a chalk-white cliff.

From Jerusalem the scene shifts to Rome, where one is confronted with Caligula, Claudius, and Nero—the three "wild beasts"—in that order. When in the end Nero is stabbed to death by his slave, the Lamb has gained the victory. Again Strindberg has used Cartaphilus, the wander-ing Jew, as a figurative link in the drama.

In certain of the fifteen scenes Strindberg is shown in better form than in the two preceding plays of this cycle. Caiphas' interrogation of the disciple John before the High Council is an effective scene, particularly because of the retorts of John, which throughout are of a different dimen-sion than the questions asked. The treatment of the three "wild beasts" has occasionally tempted Strindberg to the point of engaging in rollicking farce. When Messalina, the wife of Emperor Claudius, quite unexpectedly speaks of Silius as "my husband," Claudius bursts out: "Do you go and get married without asking my permission?" And Messalina replies: "Y-e-s!"—Then Claudius says: "I must say you are an amusing woman, Messalina. . . . And I forgive you.—Go then, my children, and enjoy yourselves. . . . Narcissus will play with me."

The scenes with the madman Caligula, who worships his own image, and with Nero, who roves about in the catacombs, possess a certain dramatic power.

Christ was performed together with the two other plays in this cycle at the Civic Theater in Hanover in 1922. When in 1929 the play was given as a religious drama in the Church of St. George in Hamburg, with multicolored lighting effects from projectors, without any proper scenic décor, the setting won acclaim. When the drama was presented as a mystery play in Cologne in 1947, a critic made special mention of the fact that the Protestant Strindberg—contrary to the Roman Catholic faithful in the Oberammergau passion play—tactfully had Christ performed unseen, without being embodied physically on the stage—a practice that always is likely to present a delicate and difficult problem.

GUNNAR OLLÉN

Translator's Preface

When toward the end of the nineteenth century the German journalist Georg Bröckner submitted to August Strindberg a questionnaire in which he, among other questions, inquired which social reform the Swedish author would most like to see brought about, his answer was: disarmament. At the time that the International Peace Conference was about to be convened at The Hague in 1899, he had seriously contemplated composing a series of dramas depicting events in the history of the world that were of universal significance and had had an influence upon the fate of humanity.

The first one of these world historical dramas, dealing with Martin Luther and the beginning of the Reformation, was written in 1903. The distinguished Strindberg scholar and critic Erik Hedén speaks of this drama in his biography *Strindberg** as one of his most pulsating and colorful dramas. While other critics may not share this judgment, I myself am of the opinion that the first act is one of the most fascinating and imaginative expositions of what is to come, firmly establishing the character of the protagonist as well as that of his austere and iron-willed parents. I find many of the other characters completely believable also; and, through the role of Johannes Faust, Strindberg compassionately makes a plea for justice to both sides in the conflict, just as he has Luther denounce those of his followers who in their excessive zeal and fanaticism try to bring about reform through violence.

* Erik Hedén: *Strindberg*. Bokförlaget Nutiden, Stockholm, 1921; Tidens Förlag, Stockholm, 1926.

The Nightingale of Wittenberg is a play of conflict between the spiritual and material forces in the world—a battle that is still going on at a far from slackened pace.

Moses is, as Gunnar Ollén points out, merely a paraphrasing of the Old Testament, retouched and augmented by the dramatist. But again this play brings out starkly the unceasing strife that for centuries has existed in that part of the world, and still continues.

Hellas, or *Socrates*, is likewise a play about strife. But here the conflict is one of mind as well as between the rival states of Sparta and Athens and between Greeks and the peoples of Asia Minor, each with a different morality and philosophy of life. It also reveals the towering common sense of Socrates and his disciple Plato, brought out by Strindberg in persuasive dialogue, and Socrates' foreboding of the decline and overthrow of their pagan deities, prophesying the coming of a new and greater god.

This drama has much in it that both is moving and holds the interest, ending as it does with the death of the wise and lovable philosopher. After having been falsely and maliciously imprisoned as an enemy of the State of Athens, he chooses to die and drains a potion of the poisonous hemlock while his devoted friend Plato comes to visit him in his cell. He prefers death to the prostituting and denying of his conscience and beliefs.

In *The Lamb and the Beast*, or *Christ*, Strindberg—without embodying Christ in the play, nor having his voice heard—chronicles the history of Christianity from the birth of the Saviour to his death at Golgotha. The three monstrous beasts who during the early days of the spreading of the gospel cruelly and ruthlessly threatened His followers with death and extinction, are Claudius, Caligula, and Nero.

There are scenes in this play that are absorbing and genuinely stirring, as well as some that are satirically amusing. Nothing that the great Swedish dramatist ever wrote was lacking in interest. To my mind these four plays—while not among the very best or most famous works that he wrote for the stage—can nevertheless not be neglected. It is for that reason that I am making them available in translation to American and English readers.

ARVID PAULSON

THE NIGHTINGALE
OF WITTENBERG
(LUTHER)

Persons in the Play:

FATHER LUTHER
MOTHER LUTHER
MARTIN LUTHER
JACOB, his brother
DOCTOR JOHANNES (FAUST)
FREDERICK THE WISE, Elector of Saxony
STAUPITZ, prior of the Augustinian Monastery
SPALATIN, the Elector's chancellor
ALEXIUS, a student
FRANZ VON SICKINGEN
ULRICH VON HUTTEN
ERASMUS
REUCHLIN
DOCTOR KARLSTADT
MELANCHTHON
HANS SACHS, the mastersinger
LUCAS CRANACH, the painter
BERLEPSCH, commandant of Wartburg Castle
CONSTANTIA PEUTINGER
EMPEROR CHARLES V
ALEANDER, papal legate
AMSDORFF
SCHURFF
THE SOLDIER
THE JOURNEYMAN
THE SCHOOLMASTER
LEONHARD KAISER
THE DOMINICAN (JOHANNES DIEZEL)
THE STEWARD OF WARTBURG CASTLE
Students, monks,
printers, court attendants, etc.

The Scenes of the Play:

Act I

Luther's childhood home, 1492.

Act II

Scene 1: *The library of the Elector in Wittenberg*
Scene 2: *The attic outside Alexius' student chamber*
Scene 3: *Luther's own home*

Act III

Scene 1: *In the monastery*
Scene 2: *At Franz von Sickingen's at Ebernburg*
Scene 3: *At the Elector's of Saxony*
Scene 4: *The portal of the palace chapel at Wittenberg*
Scene 5: *Viridarium. Peutinger's garden at Augsburg*
Scene 6: *Dr. Johannes' laboratory in Leipzig*

Act IV

Outside the Elster Gate at Wittenberg

Act V

Scene 1: *The reception room outside the Council Chamber at Worms*
Scene 2: *The home of Luther's parents at Möhra.*
Scene 3: *At Wartburg Castle*

Act I

Luther's childhood home, 1492.
Martin and Jacob are standing by the stove reading in their
schoolbooks.

MARTIN: *Hic, haec, hoc,* genitive *hejus.* . . .

JACOB: *Hujus* is the genitive.

MARTIN: That's what it says in the book; but it must be wrong. . . . You say: *is, ea, id,* genitive *ejus,* don't you?

JACOB: You must say *hujus,* Martin, because that's the way the book has it.

MARTIN: I am not going to say it—I don't want it to be *hujus!* No—no!

JACOB: Then you'll get a thrashing again. . . .

MARTIN: I'll get one anyhow . . . even if I know my lesson by heart. Yesterday father heard me in my lesson in Donatus, and I knew it perfectly at home—but when the schoolmaster asked me to recite the passage in class, I couldn't remember it . . . and then he struck me till I bled. And when I came home, mother beat me because I had been beaten in school! She said it was shameful of me. . . . But I say it's an injustice and the schoolmaster is inhuman. I don't care about the pain—but the shame of it, the shame!

JACOB: Well, why don't you study then, Martin?

MARTIN: What's the good of it? He'll say I don't know my lesson, no matter what I say. But you see, Jacob, the worst of it is that he has threatened to beat me in front of his daughters—and that is shameful. But if he does that today, I'll go and drown myself in the lake, or set fire to the house . . . yes, I'll burn up the village, the forest, the whole universe—there is nothing good in the world—no justice— not that much!

(*He snaps his fingers, and flings the book under the cabinet.*)
Jacob, let's run away—out into the forest—and become
highwaymen! Then we can plunder the schoolmaster's
garden. . . .

JACOB: No, I don't want to because then the soldiers
will come and hurt us.

MARTIN: You are a coward, Jacob! But I am not
afraid. And if I can't be a brigand, then I'd want to be a
shoemaker's apprentice. It is better than to sit and read
such stupidities as this. *Hujus?* I am certain it should be
hejus—but some old fossil of a teacher made a mistake once
upon a time, and so they just let it stay that way! And now
I am going to go to school no longer. . . . I am on my own
now. . . .

JACOB: What are you going to do, Martin? What are
you going to be?

MARTIN: I am going to be a king.

JACOB: You are out of your mind, Martin.

MARTIN: If I were a sorcerer, I would conjure forth a
feast on the table. I would like to have a goose, stuffed with
prunes. . . .

JACOB: You mustn't speak like that, Martin. You must
not mention the word sorcery.

MARTIN: Must not! Who can forbid me to say what
I want to? Haven't I been given a tongue to speak with?
Haven't I a mind of my own—a will of my own?

JACOB: Quiet! Father is coming. . . .

MARTIN: No—he is down in the mine; and mother is
over at the landgrave's at the castle, helping with the
washing.

JACOB: Then it must be the schoolmaster who is out
for a walk.

MARTIN: The schoolmaster isn't human. . . .

JACOB: Pick up the book and start reading, in case anyone comes. . . .

MARTIN: I could never be that false.

JACOB: Please, Martin—please pick up your book. . . .

MARTIN: No, no, no! I've told you I won't do it!

JACOB: Well, then I'll do it. . . .

(*He crawls under the cabinet and retrieves the book.*)

MARTIN (*By the window, looking out*): I believe it *is* the schoolmaster who is coming. I see someone. . . . Give me the book!

JACOB: Suppose he wants to hear us in our lessons. . . .

MARTIN: Then we'll be chastised, of course. . . . And have his girls look on while he does it! No—I am going to say *hujus*—even if it is wrong. . . . I'll read over my lesson, but I don't think it'll be of much use.—Jacob, do you think it would help if I made a sacrifice?

JACOB: Made a sacrifice? For what?

MARTIN: So that I would know my lesson, of course.

JACOB: What have we that we could sacrifice?

MARTIN: I'll sacrifice my bread for breakfast—I have it in my pocket. I'll put it behind the stove—where I can get at it again, in case I should change my mind.

JACOB: It would be better to give it to some beggar; we have so many coming by here.

MARTIN: Yes, let's do that. . . . Oh, if only some poor man would come around now. . . . Oh, if only a beggar would come. . . . Let us pray to Mary, Mother of God, that she send us a beggar!

JACOB: Then you might just as well pray that you will know your lesson. . . .

MARTIN: No, you have to make some sort of effort yourself too—otherwise it seems like begging.—Be quiet now—he is coming in. . . .   (*He starts to read*) *Hic—haec—hoc*—genitive *hujus*. . . .

THE JOURNEYMAN   (*Enters. He carries a knapsack and a heavy stick*): I don't know whether you are schoolboys or young apprentices—but . . . could you put me up for the night?

MARTIN   (*To Jacob*): It wasn't he!

THE JOURNEYMAN (*Facetiously, to himself*): Then, with your permission, stranger, make yourself at home, and sit down at table!   (*He sits down.*)
Where are your mother and father?

MARTIN: They are away.

THE JOURNEYMAN: Have you any food in the house?

MARTIN: Here is some bread. . . .

THE JOURNEYMAN: Let's have it!—Yes, I see it is a bread . . . that you don't want to eat yourself, you little rascal. But it's bread just the same. . . . Have you any butter?

MARTIN: We have no butter.

THE JOURNEYMAN: Yes—times are hard. . . . I am a licensed journeyman in the silversmith trade—from Nuremberg—and I know. Anyhow, I'll eat it. And while I, with your permission, am eating this stale bread, I am going to hear you in your lesson, if you don't mind.—So: one, two, three, now we'll bite the bit off the key. . . . You, Kunz, who seem to be the smarter of you two. . . .

MARTIN: My name is Martin.

THE JOURNEYMAN: To me you are Kunz, for that's what I want it to be. And my will is law, as long as I have this thick stick in my hand and as long as no one who is stronger comes to your defense. Answer me now: who is emperor of Germany today?

MARTIN: Frederick the Third.

THE JOURNEYMAN: That's both right and wrong, for his name is Frederick III as Roman emperor, Frederick IV as king of Germany, and as archduke of Austria he is called

Frederick V. A queer body, eh?—Now there, you Heinz, what's the name of the pope in Rome?

JACOB: My name is Jacob.

THE JOURNEYMAN: But you are not the pope—and so you didn't answer my question. Kunz, rise when I question you! What's the name of the new pope in Rome?

MARTIN: His name is Alexander.

THE JOURNEYMAN: That's correct. His name is Alexander VI Borgia, and he is the biggest sow that ever lived. I know, for I have been in Rome. . . . Now, Heinz, which year of grace are we living in?

JACOB: In the year of our Lord 1492.

THE JOURNEYMAN: Quite correct, and—note this well —it is a year to remember. However, when you know something about the emperor and the pope, then you know how the land lies. . . . Somebody is knocking at the door. . . . Come in!

THE SOLDIER (*Enters*): Can I get lodging here?

THE JOURNEYMAN: By all means, soldier. Come in and sit down. . . .

THE SOLDIER   (*Seats himself*): Have you anything to drink?

THE JOURNEYMAN: No, not a drop. These are bad times.

THE SOLDIER: I can't complain.

THE JOURNEYMAN: I am speaking for myself—I am a silversmith. . . .

THE SOLDIER: And I am speaking for *myself*—I am a soldier.

THE JOURNEYMAN: . . . and all the gold and silver goes to Rome—so there is nothing left for our trade.

THE SOLDIER: I am just on my way to Rome, and I am glad to hear there is plenty of gold there.

THE JOURNEYMAN: Oh, so you are going to Rome?—

What a silly fool he is—the new pope they have just elected.

THE SOLDIER: What are you talking about! We've never had such a generous pope before!

THE JOURNEYMAN: That may be, but he is the brother-in-law of his own son and is married to his own daughter.

THE SOLDIER: What have I to do with that!—But if there ever was a real blackguard, it's the emperor. There he sits, reading books about herbs and vermin, while the Hungarians are in Vienna and the Turks are invading Hungary. There is something rotten in the air—and if we don't get a change soon, the whole of Europe will go to hell.

THE JOURNEYMAN: Yes, and it all has its roots in Rome—all of it. . . .

THE SOLDIER: It doesn't come from Rome, for that's where I am going.

THE JOURNEYMAN: And I have *been* in Rome.

THE SOLDIER: Well, I don't care about that. I want to see it myself! What I haven't seen myself, I don't believe— it doesn't exist for me.

THE JOURNEYMAN: And what a lot of things there are to see in Rome! Oy, oy, oy!

THE SOLDIER: Yes, and I want to see it! I don't want to hear about it. . . . I want to see it for myself!

(*There is a knock at the door*)

THE JOURNEYMAN: Somebody is knocking at the door. . . . Come in!

THE DOMINICAN (*Enters*): Can I get a room overnight here?

THE JOURNEYMAN: Come and sit down, Brother, if you please.

THE DOMINICAN: Peace, good people.

THE SOLDIER: Where do you come from, Brother?

THE DOMINICAN: I come from Rome.

THE SOLDIER: Oh, for heaven's sake. . . . Tell us about

it, tell us! I am just on my way there. Is it true that they carouse like swine there? That the cardinals are giving gay parties at night, with nude women, and that the pope. . . .

THE DOMINICAN: That's a lie—it's all a lie. . . .

THE SOLDIER: Imagine, how people in this world can lie. . . .

THE JOURNEYMAN: Lie, did you say? Haven't I been there myself and seen it with my own eyes? Hasn't the pope a child by his own daughter?

THE DOMINICAN: It's a lie—a lie. Alexander VI is a holy man, and he'll do more to extend the power of the Church than anyone before him. But he has a son, Cesare Borgia, who is a notorious scoundrel, and you have probably confused him with the father.

THE JOURNEYMAN: No, I am not confused at all. I have never heard of anything so brazen in my life. . . . How can a priest have children? Has he the right to that?

THE DOMINICAN: That's journeyman's lies! . . . But *maxima debetur pueris reverentia*—please be good enough to change the subject of conversation in the presence of these children.

THE SOLDIER: Yes, but can it really be lies—not that I care, but just the same. . . . .

THE DOMINICAN: It's pure, unadulterated lies, spread by Hussites and heretics!

THE JOURNEYMAN: Well, if that isn't the . . .

THE DOMINICAN: Keep your mouth shut, journeyman, or I'll. . . .

THE SOLDIER: But tell me—there is much to do in Rome, isn't there? There are Frenchmen and Turks. . . .

THE JOURNEYMAN (*Burying his head in his hands*): He says it's lies. . . . Lies, he says. . . . Can you imagine. . . ? And Huss—the great Huss who will never be forgotten. . . .

THE DOMINICAN: Huss was an execrable ass—and

that's why he was burned like so much dust! You had best be careful there, journeyman! . . . Boys, can you get me a horse, do you think?

MARTIN: No, we have no horse.

THE DOMINICAN: I asked you if you could *get* me one. If you had had one, you wouldn't have had to *get* me one, you simpleton.

MARTIN: We don't own one, and I can't get you one.

THE DOMINICAN: Listen to him! He has what I call a big snout!—I must have a horse.

THE SOLDIER: It's going to be a little hard to find one here in poverty-stricken Mansfeld, I'm afraid. . . . I thought I heard someone at the door. . . . Come in!

> (*The Dominican winces.*)
> (*The Wanderer, a slight, graying man, enters.*)

THE SOLDIER: Come in and sit down.

> (*The Wanderer seats himself.*)

THE DOMINICAN: Where do you come from?

THE WANDERER: From Wittenberg.

THE DOMINICAN: Was the Elector there?

THE WANDERER: Yes . . . he was there. . . . H'm— haven't we seen each other before?

THE DOMINICAN: No, never!

THE WANDERER: I thought. . . .

THE SOLDIER: What news from Wittenberg?

THE WANDERER: From Wittenberg itself there is nothing of special interest. But I heard a story there—a sort of fairy tale. . . . You gentlemen remember a seafarer from Genoa who sailed westward from Spain in an attempt to find the way to India? You remember, eh?

THE DOMINICAN: Yes—some idiot who thought he could come east by traveling west. . . .

THE WANDERER: Yes—just that idiot. . . .

THE SOLDIER: An obstinate fool bent on doing away

with himself. . . . And who took aboard with him a cargo of convicts in order to be rid of the whole collection of them at one time.

THE WANDERER: So-oh?

(*The old man seems to be growing in stature as the conversation progresses.*)

THE DOMINICAN: Have you any idea where I can get a horse?

THE WANDERER: No—so much the less as the only remaining horse in the adjoining village was stolen this morning and was found ridden to death in the woods near Eckartsbühle.

(*The Dominican gives a start.*)

THE WANDERER: You asked for news. Brother Dominican, have you heard of Savonarola in Florence?

THE JOURNEYMAN: Savonarola? The goldsmith? I know him!

THE DOMINICAN (*To The Wanderer*): I know who the Dominican Savonarola is.

THE WANDERER: Who is he, then?

THE DOMINICAN: He is a louse, a dirty dog!

THE WANDERER: No, he is anything but that!

THE SOLDIER: If I could only get something to drink!

THE JOURNEYMAN: I say the same!

THE WANDERER: Are you gentlemen thirsty? May I offer you a glass of wine?

THE DOMINICAN: How can you do that?

THE WANDERER (*Produces four glasses and a bottle of wine*): Here you see how it is done.

THE SOLDIER (*Drinks*): This is what I call wine!

THE JOURNEYMAN: You are right. . . . This is wine, Mr. Wanderer. . . .

THE DOMINICAN: Magnificent!

(*The Wanderer spills his wine on the table.*)

THE DOMINICAN: It looks as if you had drawn a map on the table.

THE WANDERER: Does it really look like a map to you? If it does, do you know what land it is?

THE DOMINICAN: It doesn't look like any land I know.

THE WANDERER: That is because it is an unknown land! Now let us light a few candles and look closer at this land. (*He brings out a candelabrum and lights the candles.*)

THE SOLDIER: You certainly think of everything, sir!

THE WANDERER: Now be so good as to look at my map, good sirs. . . . (*All regard the wine spot on the table.*) What do you see, Brother Dominican?

THE DOMINICAN: It looks like a group of islands. . . .

THE WANDERER: Do you see any ships at anchor there?

THE JOURNEYMAN: I see three ships. . . .

THE SOLDIER: A caravel. . . .

THE DOMINICAN: I see a shore with palms, and naked human beings with red skin. . . . What's this I see here? A soldier, dressed like a Spaniard, kneeling. . . . His hands are clasping his sword hilt—and, wait a moment. . . . (*He puts on his spectacles.*) I see a man holding a banner aloft. . . . What flag is that, soldier?

THE SOLDIER: Let me see. . . . That's the banner of the Castilians!

THE WANDERER: Yes, that's right—the flag of the Castilians. . . . And who is the soldier?

THE DOMINICAN: Is it Columbus? Is it?

(*There is a silence.*)

THE WANDERER: Do you know the insignia of our gracious emperor?

ALL: No. . . .

THE WANDERER: If I put my question in a different way, I should get the answer. Young Martin over there—

tell me the vowels in the German language. . . .

MARTIN: A—e—i—o—u.

THE WANDERER: Those are the insignia of the German emperor. . . . The lad didn't know—but just the same he gave the correct answer. . . . And they stand for: Austria est imperare orbi universo.—Translate that, Jacob!

JACOB: Austria shall rule the entire universe.

THE WANDERER: That is right—and it is right and proper. The whole world—the known and the unknown world. . . . And it will come to pass under his great-grandson . . . remember that!

(*He wipes the table dry.*)

And that's the end!

THE DOMINICAN: Who are you?

THE WANDERER: I know who *you* are, what you have done, and what you plan to do. . . . I know that today two planets have come in conflict with each other and that two fates have in this room entered into conjunction with each other, in this room.—Who am I? H'm. . . . But you are Johannes Diezel!

THE DOMINICAN: That's a lie!

THE WANDERER: A lie! That seems to be the only word in your vocabulary! And therefore you, and just you, shall—as a punishment—be the means of bringing about the truth. You, the lackey of Antichrist, shall bring about the fall of Antichrist—and you, the impostor, the swindler and oppressor, shall give us freedom—against your will!

THE DOMINICAN: May the Lord chastise you, Satan!

THE WANDERER: And punish you, murderer!

THE DOMINICAN (*Springs up*): If you are not the devil himself, then you must be Doctor F. . . .

THE WANDERER: You now know who I am, yet you don't know me. But you *will* know me some day! Go on ahead now—and I will follow you!

THE DOMINICAN (*Drags himself toward the door. To the Soldier and the Journeyman*): Don't sit at the same table with this sorcerer. He has sold his soul to the devil. . . .

THE SOLDIER: The devil! He is the one power I don't want to fight! (*He rises.*)

THE JOURNEYMAN (*Gets up from his seat, ready to depart*): Wizards and I have never mixed well. . . .

(*He returns to the table and swallows his drink of wine.*)
(*The Wanderer gathers his belongings and returns to his original stature.*)
(*The Soldier, the Dominican, and the Journeyman leave, walking backward to the door and crossing themselves in the direction of the Wanderer.*)

THE WANDERER: Children, promise me not to speak of what has taken place or what has been said here. ·

MARTIN: I promise.

THE WANDERER: Your hand on that!

MARTIN: I give you my hand and my word.

THE WANDERER (*To Jacob*): You are a weak vessel, and I don't want to bruise you. . . . Farewell!

(*He leaves.*)

MARTIN: Are you frightened, Jacob?

JACOB: Yes, I am! They were bad men!

MARTIN: I liked the magician best, for he spoke with earnestness.

JACOB: God forgive you and help you, Martin!

MARTIN: Yes, if he only would, so that I'd know my lesson and be saved from an unjust beating. . . . For it was unjust of mother to strike me the other day, so that I bled—just for the sake of a nut—you remember, Jacob!

JACOB: Yes, I remember. . . . But hadn't you taken the nut?

MARTIN: No! I say no—no! Didn't I find the nut afterward?

JACOB: Why didn't you tell mother so at once?

MARTIN: Why?—Would I have dared to tell mother that she lied? Then father would have beaten the life out of me!

JACOB: One must have forbearance with one's parents. . . .

MARTIN: Why? Why?

JACOB: You always ask so many questions, Martin.

MARTIN: Yes, I want to know why things are this way or that way; I want to know in order to be able to obey, to do the right thing.

JACOB: Be still now—father and mother are coming. . . .

MARTIN: Now we'll have another one of those scenes —I can feel it coming. . . .

JACOB: Read in your book and don't give any short answers. . . .

MARTIN: Yes, if I don't answer and give them the truth, I'd be a liar, I'd be a mute, a hypocrite! And I don't want to be that!

JACOB: Quiet! Now father throws down his load of wood on the slope. . . . He is in a bad temper when he does that!

MARTIN: It seems to me he is always in a bad temper! And so is mother.

JACOB: Be quiet now, Martin, and behave. . . .

(*Father Luther enters; he carries a wood ax in his hand.*)
(*Mother Luther comes in with a bucket and a board for beating clothes.*)

FATHER LUTHER   (*Jerks off his shoes*): Look, Margreta, there is blood in my shoes today again. . . .

MOTHER LUTHER: You should see my hands! And all for the sake of our ungrateful children.

FATHER LUTHER (*To the boys*): Have you been studying your lessons?

JACOB: Yes, we know our lessons.

FATHER LUTHER: I asked if you had studied them. If you know them is something you can't tell until the schoolmaster has heard you. It is a grace to know your lesson; it's a reward—and that's why good children always know their lessons, while bad children never know theirs—even if they have a good brain and are ever so diligent. . . . I can see your tongue is itching to say something, Martin—but don't say it. To be silent, to listen, and obey—that is what children should do. . . .

MOTHER LUTHER: And above all—they should be honest, Martin!

MARTIN: I am honest.

MOTHER LUTHER: He who steals is not honest. . . .

MARTIN: I have not stolen, mother.

MOTHER LUTHER: To think that I should have a child that both steals and lies!

MARTIN: I have neither stolen nor lied. . . . I swear by the Holy Trinity!

MOTHER LUTHER: And he takes an oath on it, too! I'll give you something for that before you go to bed tonight! I'll give you something!

FATHER LUTHER: What's this? What's this you have been doing on the table here?   (*Silence.*)
Martin, what have you been doing on the table? There is a large spot here!

MARTIN: I haven't been at the table. . . .

FATHER LUTHER: You turn red in the face? Then you are lying!

MARTIN: I can turn red from anger, can't I? When you suspect me unjustly.

FATHER LUTHER: You talk back, you little rascal!—I

think it would be better if I chopped off your head—then I wouldn't have to see the executioner do it. What have you been doing on the table?

MARTIN: Nothing! And if you beat me for nothing, I'll go and hang myself!

JACOB (*As Father Luther goes toward Martin with clenched fist*): Don't touch him! He hasn't done anything!

FATHER LUTHER: Is it you who have done it?

JACOB: No—I didn't do it!

FATHER LUTHER: Are you trying to tell me it got there by itself?

JACOB: No. . . .

FATHER LUTHER: Then answer me! But don't lie!

JACOB: We have had strangers here. . . .

FATHER LUTHER: So—you have had company. Could it have been gentle folk? And did you have anything to offer them? Perhaps you had some Rhine wine—and then spilled it on the table? . . .

JACOB: Yes, they brought wine with them. . . and then one of them, who was a doctor, drew a map of some strange country in the wine . . . and they said something about a banner. . . the banner of Castile. . . .

FATHER LUTHER: Go out in the woodshed, mother, and get the flogging stick!

MOTHER LUTHER: Yes—if it's for Martin; for it's he who teaches his brother to lie.

MARTIN: Jacob doesn't lie!

FATHER LUTHER: You want me to believe that this cock-and-bull story of his is the truth?—Now—you tell me just what has happened here!

MARTIN: I can't do it! I have promised to say nothing!

MOTHER LUTHER: Just listen to him!

FATHER LUTHER: He is possessed by a demon, that's

what he is! But I'll drive it out of him! I know how to do it. . . .

MARTIN: We had visitors here in the house. . . . They drank wine and spilled on the table. . . . That's all I can tell you—I can't say anything more, for I have given my word not to speak. And a vow is given to be kept. . . .

FATHER LUTHER: Go after the stick, mother—then I'll keep *my* promise!

MOTHER LUTHER: Yes—but not for Jacob!

FATHER LUTHER: First the one, then the other!—Have you ever heard anything like it! A map, drawn with wine—and of a strange land! Hurry up, mother!

MOTHER LUTHER: I'm going. . . . But not Jacob—he is innocent. . . .

MARTIN: And so am I. And the nut you chastised me for, I found. I threw it in the fire and asked God to put a curse on it so that no tree would grow from it and bring misfortune to some human creature.

FATHER LUTHER: These words are not his own! It's the devil speaking through him! You'll end on the executioner's block or be burnt at the stake!—What are you waiting for, mother?

(*Mother Luther goes toward the door.*)

THE SCHOOLMASTER   (*Enters excitedly*): God's peace on this house, good people! Send the boys out into the kitchen. . . . I have great news for you—and good news!

FATHER LUTHER   (*His face brightens*): Sit down, master, sit down. . . .

THE SCHOOLMASTER: The boys don't have to be in school today—in view of the importance of the day. The Holy Father is being crowned in Rome today, and all Christendom partakes in the joyous celebration! Out, boys, and play!—No chastisement for you today!

(*Martin and Jacob go into the kitchen.*)

THE SCHOOLMASTER: General amnesty!

FATHER LUTHER: Well—boys! Yes! I think they ought to have a beating even when they don't deserve it—just to get used to the injustices in the world—the way I have had to.

THE SCHOOLMASTER: No, father Hans, they should not, for then they would lose faith in justice—and they would turn into demons. And speaking of justice, the landgrave has now given you justice and has granted you the two smelting furnaces and sealed the bargain.

FATHER LUTHER: You don't say!

THE SCHOOLMASTER: Yes, and now you don't have to chop any more wood!

FATHER LUTHER: Do you hear that, mother, I have been given two smelting furnaces. . . .

MOTHER LUTHER: Yes, thank God and praise the Lord!—And it was about time. . . .

THE SCHOOLMASTER: That's not the way to speak when you receive a grant. . . . Don't come with the same remark when I bring you the other gift now!—Well, our gracious Mrs. Cotta in Eisenach has offered to take Martin into her home and to keep him in school there.

MOTHER LUTHER: Martin? Not Jacob!

THE SCHOOLMASTER: No, she likes Esau better than Jacob—and that is something you can't do anything about. But you can't deny that Martin has the best head—and he can sing, too. . . .

FATHER LUTHER: He has a big mouth, that he has. . . . And he can lie like a horse thief.

THE SCHOOLMASTER: I have never noticed that.

MOTHER LUTHER: And he steals, too. . . .

THE SCHOOLMASTER: That's a lie! You are speaking of that nut, aren't you? Well, he didn't take it, for I was here and saw when he found it.

FATHER LUTHER: You saw him . . . ? But you don't expect us, his parents, to ask him to forgive us?

THE SCHOOLMASTER: That is what we call a *casus conscientiae,* a question of conscience, which I can't undertake to solve for you. At any rate, you will be rid of him now, and that's about time, for here he would only come to harm.—Well, and now we have a new pope, as I mentioned! What do you think of a Borgia being elected pope?

FATHER LUTHER: Is it true what they say?

THE SCHOOLMASTER: Yes, it is, it's true. The incest has been proved, and there has been some whispering about a little murder also. But in this day of enlightenment, you can't demand too much of people!—Well, everything will adjust itself. . . .

MOTHER LUTHER: They say he is Antichrist himself, and I am afraid we are going to have hard times from now on. . . .

THE SCHOOLMASTER: Yes, conditions are strange, but we can't do anything to change them—we, who have no voice. . . . Well, did the magician visit *you,* too?

FATHER LUTHER: Magician?

THE SCHOOLMASTER: Yes—he was down in the village, at the shoemaker's, drawing maps on the table, in wine, talking a lot of nonsense. . . .

FATHER LUTHER: Drawing maps with wine . . . ?

THE SCHOOLMASTER: Yes—there is so much of that sort of blabber and hocus-pocus going on. . . . I heard he came here, too.

FATHER LUTHER: Mother, tell the boys they can go outside and play. . . wherever they want to go. . . . In all my life I have never heard anything to equal this!—Well, we learn as long as we live. . . .

(*Mother Luther goes into the kitchen.*)

THE SCHOOLMASTER (*To Mother Luther*): Speak **a**

nice word to Martin now! Just one word! It will do more
good than any beating!

FATHER LUTHER: What we don't live to see!

THE SCHOOLMASTER: But here comes the real climax!
The emperor is dying; and with Maximilian as emperor, the
Germans will get Burgundy and the Netherlands, perhaps
even Spain!

FATHER LUTHER: What we don't live to see! That's
all I can say. . . .

THE SCHOOLMASTER: Yes, what we have to live to see!

End of Act One

Act II

Scene I

The library of the Elector at Wittenberg.
At a table, right, are seated Diezel and Ulrich von Hutten
(incognito). At another table, left, sit Doctor Johannes,
Doctor Luther; Staupitz (dressed in the garb of an Augus-
tinian monk) and Spalatin are standing down stage, speak-
ing in undertones.

STAUPITZ: People are beginning to read books now,
Spalatin. . . . It doesn't hurt.

SPALATIN: And the things they say in these books!—
That fellow Erasmus is a regular horse rake that scrapes
off both lice and hide.

STAUPITZ: And the monks are being flayed right and
left. To tell the truth, I am ashamed of the garb I am
wearing when I hear and read these stories about life in the
monasteries. Have you heard the latest one about a horse
theft and a murder?

SPALATIN: Yes. . . . Monastic life has become per-
meated with rottenness, and Boccaccio, the Italian, was
aware of that already a hundred years ago. . . . Now that
this book has been printed you may be sure it's being read!
Look at that fellow over there at that table—he is reading
him now! And he is enjoying himself evidently!
                    (*He indicates the table on the right.*)

STAUPITZ: Who is he—that man?

SPALATIN: I don't know. Anybody is welcome here...
but I understand he is a close friend of Sickingen.—Have
you read Boccaccio?

STAUPITZ: No—it is a book that has a very bad reputation. . . .

SPALATIN: . . . and nevertheless read with pleasure by the Holy Father himself!

STAUPITZ: If there is any truth in what he writes, he has a right to say it.

SPALATIN: Do you know who the Dominican is over there—to the right?

STAUPITZ: No—but I believe his name is Diezel or Tiezel. . . and he is studying the decretals. . . . Here the knives are being sharpened, while I turn the grindstone.

SPALATIN: What do you, personally, think of monastic life, friend Staupitz?

STAUPITZ: As a place for sick people the monastery has its good influence; it is no place for a healthy person!

SPALATIN: And as seats for higher learning, they are superfluous now that the university has been opened. . . .

STAUPITZ: Yes, exactly! You know, Spalatin, between ourselves, religion—as a profession—can almost degenerate into a vice! And I am longing to get away from it. . . . The Elector is coming. . . .

SPALATIN: The kindly Elector who collects relics with one hand and caresses heretics with the other. . .

STAUPITZ: Heretics?

SPALATIN: Well, there is something of the heretic in all of us, don't you think?—No, it was not the Elector. . . .

STAUPITZ: Who is that swarthy scholar over there at the corner of the table, to the left?

SPALATIN: I think his name is Doctor Johannes—and he has a certain renown for being a—a magician!

STAUPITZ: No, I mean the one sitting next to him.

SPALATIN: Oh, he! He is a young man who just received his doctor's degree. . . his name is Luther. I don't know anything about him otherwise. . . .

STAUPITZ: What is he reading?

SPALATIN: I think he is interested in jurisprudence. . . .
The Elector is coming. . . .

THE ELECTOR   (*Enters. All present rise but seat them-selves again at a gesture from the Elector*): Well, my good
Spalatin. . . . You, as the source of all wisdom, tell me—
how far has Columbus penetrated over there in the new
world?

SPALATIN: The last news is that Columbus has not
found the way to India.

THE ELECTOR: He has failed then! But where is he—
and what is the unknown land he has discovered?

SPALATIN: He has discovered an entire new world.

THE ELECTOR: But where could that be?

SPALATIN: Well, that's just the question! Westward
from Spain! But that's where the end of the world was said
to be. . . .

THE ELECTOR: Is there any human being who can explain this? Is there any mortal who can give enlightenment
on this?

DOCTOR JOHANNES   (*Respectfully rising from his seat*):
Forgive me for being so bold, but since Your Grace's question is made at large, I beg you to permit me to answer it.

THE ELECTOR: By all means!

DOCTOR JOHANNES: Christopher Columbus is now at
the opposite side of the earth.

THE ELECTOR: Has the earth more sides than one?

DOCTOR JOHANNES: It has numberless sides, because
it is round like a globe.

THE ELECTOR: What's this I hear? Show me—and
prove it to me!

DOCTOR JOHANNES   (*Brings out a globe of the earth
from under the table*): This is the shape of the earth. . . .

THE ELECTOR: Are you sane?

DOCTOR JOHANNES: And the new world appears some-what like this.

(*He describes by encircling a part of the globe with his index finger.*)

THE ELECTOR: How do you know?

DOCTOR JOHANNES: It has been known since pre-historic times, but no one has wanted to believe it. Yes—such is faith!

THE ELECTOR: Continue. . . .

DOCTOR JOHANNES: During my first visit in the Vat-ican, I came across a manuscript by a fairly unknown Greek named Agesianax. . . .

THE ELECTOR: Never heard of him! Have you, Spala-tin?

SPALATIN: I know the name, but that is all. . . .

DOCTOR JOHANNES: This learned Greek had noticed the dark, map-like images on the moon—and from their somewhat misshapen contours arrived at the conclusion that they were the reflexion of the continents of the earth. How-ever, as there were regions among these he could not iden-tify, he drew the conclusion that still another continent existed on this planet, as yet undiscovered.

THE ELECTOR: I don't wish to hear any more! Take that thing away—take it away! (*To Spalatin.*) It's enough to make one lose one's mind! Tell me something else, Spala-tin . . . the university! My university at Wittenberg shall have professors in all the four faculties—and you shall pro-cure them for me. . . . And in the new chapel there I shall deposit the remains of the saints that I have been collecting for all these years. . . . Have you heard anything new from Rome, Spalatin?

SPALATIN: Yes, your noble Grace . . . but perhaps it would be best if we withdrew to the conference room? . . .

THE ELECTOR: Is it that kind of news? Very well!

(Spalatin and the Elector go into the adjoining room. Immediately afterward Spalatin returns. He gestures to Staupitz who leaves with him.)

ULRICH VON HUTTEN   *(Rises with gaiety)*: I have it now! Now we won't be unprepared, lads! Thank you, doctor, for the globe! Whether true or not—at least it is something new to be looking at the other side of the earth! And I like new ideas!—O-ho, now we'll be seeing a change! The spirits are awakening, and it is a joy to be living!

DOCTOR JOHANNES: With whom have I the honor to be . . . ?

ULRICH VON HUTTEN: No names—we have to make a name for ourselves first. . . . I am a *novus homo* and I am writing about obscure men, twilight men, shady men . . . about horse thieves and defilers of men. . . .

DIEZEL: Please be quiet in the library!

ULRICH VON HUTTEN: Who is speaking? Perhaps it would be a little difficult to know . . . perhaps the county constabulary down near Salzkammergut could more readily answer that question! Perhaps he who had his hands in somebody else's pouch will end in a sack! Perhaps the son of a goldsmith can sell the horse thief from Mansfeld forgiveness for his sins for fifty ducats!

DIEZEL: That's a lie!

DOCTOR JOHANNES: The father of lies! We have met before!

DIEZEL   *(Rises)*: I have the honor, even though I have not the honor—to know you!   *(He starts to leave.)*

ULRICH VON HUTTEN   *(Calling out after Diezel)*: He takes flight! But I shall follow you—to the court house steps, to the stocks, to the executioner's block. . . .

DIEZEL   *(Turns)*: Now I know you—and I shall pursue *you*—and first of all when you go courting. . . . When you ask for your bride's hand in marriage, I shall stand next to

her and say: Don't take that man, for he is contaminated by
morbus Gallicus. . . .When you are a guest of friends and sit
at table, I shall be present and give them warning: Don't
drink from his glass—he has the lues!

ULRICH VON HUTTEN: Yes—I have the lues . . . and I
have acquired it honestly, like a man, in open combat of
love. . . . But you got yours in a place not to be mentioned
and in a manner called *mos ferarum.* Now be on your way,
you vagrant whore, and tell your master you have met Ulrich von Hutten, direct from Steckelberg! But watch out
for the hiding places in the forest and the dark corners of
the ravine! Watch out for water courses and pillars of fire!
My arm is long and my eye is as sharp as the lynx's! Aren't
you out yet!   (*Diezel disappears speedily.*)
Forgive me, good sirs!—And now you know my secret—
which is my sad fate. . . .

DOCTOR JOHANNES: We respect your secret—it is a
secret every fourth man in Germany has to carry! Do you,
sirs, know, for instance, why we have been fortunate
enough to get a university in Wittenberg?—I shall tell you:
—because the learned professors in Leipzig became em-
broiled in a dispute over the treatment of *morbus Gallicus*
and no longer can tolerate each other in the same city!

ULRICH VON HUTTEN: It should really be called *morbus Romanus,* for it comes from Rome—as everything rotten! That's why my motto is, first and last: Rome must be
done away with! *Roma est delenda!*

DOCTOR JOHANNES: Have you, sirs, heard the latest
from Rome? They have discovered a statue in the baths
of Titus—Titus who destroyed Jerusalem—a statue of Laocoön, the Trojan priest, you know, who tried to save Troy
from the renowned wooden horse and the soldiers of the
enemy. As punishment Apollo sent two snakes that killed
the priest and his two sons. This statue, however, pleased

the Romans so much that they carried it in procession around the streets to the tolling of the temple bells.

ULRICH VON HUTTEN: That might be called portentous . . . a good omen. . . .

DOCTOR JOHANNES: You mean to say that the Romans now have a Trojan horse within their walls?

ULRICH VON HUTTEN: I hope so! And I firmly believe that Rome will fall. . . . *Roma est delenda!*—Goodbye, good sirs.   (*He leaves.*)

DOCTOR JOHANNES   (*Pushes a book in front of Luther*): Have you seen this book, doctor?

MARTIN LUTHER: No, I am studying the pandects. I am devoting myself to law.

DOCTOR JOHANNES: But look at it anyhow. . . .

MARTIN LUTHER: What is this book? Biblia? Is this the Bible? The whole Bible?

DOCTOR JOHANNES: The Scriptures complete. . . .

MARTIN LUTHER: Is it that large? All I have ever seen are the gospels and the epistles that rest on the altar. . . .

DOCTOR JOHANNES: This book holds many secrets— yes, it is a veritable book of magic.

MARTIN LUTHER: I don't believe that!

DOCTOR JOHANNES: Try it! Turn to any page at random. . . .

MARTIN LUTHER   (*Turns to one of the pages and reads*): . . . What's this? . . . "And the child Samuel ministered unto the Lord before Eli. And the word of the Lord was precious in those days; there was no open vision. . . . And the Lord called Samuel again the third time. And Samuel grew, and the Lord was with him, and did let none of his words fall on the ground. And all Israel knew that Samuel was established to be a prophet of the Lord. . . . And the Philistines took the ark of God and brought it into the house of Dagon and set it by the idol Dagon. . . . And when they arose early on the morrow, behold, Dagon was fallen upon his face to the earth before the ark of the Lord." —Yes, and there are still idols left in the world! . . . There can be no denying that! No! . . . It is strange—the resemblance between the past and what is happening today! It is as if it were written only yesterday! . . . Here we have need of a Samuel—but where can he be found? . . .

DOCTOR JOHANNES (*Places his hand on Luther's shoulder*): Here he is!

MARTIN LUTHER: Don't blaspheme! I am a man of earthly habits, full of suppressed carnal desires and with an eager lust for the things of the flesh!

DOCTOR JOHANNES: Rome is in the land of the Philistines.

MARTIN LUTHER: Say nothing evil about Rome. . . . It is a holy place—it is where God lives.

DOCTOR JOHANNES: Did live once! Antichrist lives there now!

MARTIN LUTHER: I have to see it myself! That is—if it were any concern of mine. . . .

ALEXIUS (*Enters; he is agitated, in despair*): Forgive me for disturbing you!—Martin, help me! Come with me!

MARTIN LUTHER: I haven't time. . . .

ALEXIUS: For God's sake! I am in trouble. . . .

MARTIN LUTHER: I can't help that! You have to manage your own filthy affairs. . . .

ALEXIUS: Listen to me, Martin. . . .

MARTIN LUTHER: Go away!

ALEXIUS: Where shall I go? Where?

MARTIN LUTHER: Go to hell, you swine!

ALEXIUS: You will be sorry for this some day, Martin. . . .

MARTIN LUTHER: I never do anything I need to regret. . . .

ALEXIUS: May God be merciful to you when you wake up from your unbounded selfishness!

MARTIN LUTHER: Don't be impudent! I am not selfish!
(*Alexius leaves. He is weeping.*)

MARTIN LUTHER: Are you crying, you wretch?—
(*He turns to Doctor Johannes.*)
Yes, Doctor Johannes, this is a book I should like to borrow. . . . Is it yours?

DOCTOR JOHANNES: It is mine, and you may borrow it. . . . But be careful—it is double-edged—don't cut yourself!

MARTIN LUTHER: Reading Aristotle didn't hurt me—and Martin Luther has flesh that heals easily. . . . Tell me, have we ever met before?

DOCTOR JOHANNES: Yes, in your childhood home.

MARTIN LUTHER: Oh!—Why—of course . . . it was you who drew maps in wine—and who had sold himself to the devil, they said. . . .

DOCTOR JOHANNES: I am that selfsame man, yes. . . . And do you believe that I have?

MARTIN LUTHER: Who can tell?

DOCTOR JOHANNES: Can a *Ludi magister* put faith in such drivel?—And why should the devil have to buy souls when he can get so many for nothing?

MARTIN LUTHER: Now I am going to the consistory—and afterward I am going home and read the Bible. Then I'll see whether I can profit by it. . . . Goodbye, doctor . . . we'll meet again.

DOCTOR JOHANNES: We shall always meet here.

MARTIN LUTHER: Yes! And we'll remain good friends —as long as you leave Rome alone!

End of Scene One

Scene II

The attic outside Alexius' living quarters.
In the rear, three doors are seen.
In the foreground, a table with toilet articles: brush, comb,
etc; also a bench.
Martin Luther and Doctor Karlstadt enter.

MARTIN LUTHER: Karlstadt, wait here a moment. . . .
I am going in to see Alexius—he is coming with me to Mansfeld today.

KARLSTADT: A bad egg!

MARTIN LUTHER: That sloven is out again. . . . Well,
he must be here soon!—Let us sit down here and wait. . . .
(*They seat themselves on the bench.*)

KARLSTADT: You are so excited, Martin! What's disturbing you?

MARTIN LUTHER: Didn't sleep very well—had bad
dreams—and read into the wee hours. . . .

KARLSTADT: What did you read?

MARTIN LUTHER: The Bible. . . . It's a remarkable
book, the Bible is. . . .

KARLSTADT: It is?—What is in it?

MARTIN LUTHER: Everything!

KARLSTADT: What does it say about indulgences?

MARTIN LUTHER: Indulgence is a remission of punishment, after penance.

KARLSTADT: Yes—but murder and perjury are unforgivable sins . . . that cannot be atoned for by fine or payment. . . .

MARTIN LUTHER: I have not gone into that.—No—the
Bible is something else—that book has a personal message—
a personal message for each and every one of us. It is an

awesome, a devastating book. I wish I had never seen it. . . .
I feel as if I could never again be happy.

KARLSTADT: You are a brooder, Martin. . . .

MARTIN LUTHER: No—but there is something within
me that broods. . . . Why does that Alexius keep me waiting
so long?

KARLSTADT: Your young friend has the name of being
a heedless scamp. . . .

MARTIN LUTHER: He is young . . . and I am not old.
. . . I had hoped, however, I would be able to lead him into
a new life.

KARLSTADT: When did you see him last?

MARTIN LUTHER: Yesterday—at the library. Perhaps I
was a little brusque, a little unfriendly to him. . . . I am
almost sorry for it now. . . . You know, you hear of strange
things, sometimes, in the library. . . . Yesterday I heard the
most fantastic tales—though I can't say that I believe them
entirely. . . . Is there anybody with Alexius in his room,
or. . . .

KARLSTADT: It's just a cat you hear running around
in the attic. . . .

MARTIN LUTHER: There is something eerie, something
dismal, up here. . . .

KARLSTADT: I don't notice anything strange.—But you
are in a cold sweat, Martin!

MARTIN LUTHER: Am I?

KARLSTADT: But tell me—why are you studying jurisprudence?

MARTIN LUTHER: Because father wants me to. He has
become a well-to-do alderman now, and he wants me to
seek a government office—and then he plans to get me
married off and make a respectable match. . . .

KARLSTADT: But your own liking is for the humanities,
isn't it? . . .

MARTIN LUTHER: I really don't know what I want. . . .
I am tortured by anxiety—for everything, for the future, for
what comes after the future. . . .

KARLSTADT: What *does*?

MARTIN LUTHER: Yes—if one only knew! . . . You
know, I think he must be asleep in there—I feel he is in
his room!

KARLSTADT: He couldn't possibly be!

MARTIN LUTHER   (*Gets up from the bench and walks
toward Alexius' door*): What's this? . . . The door has been
lifted off its hinges—and—the lock is broken! . . . I must go
inside and see. . . .

DOCTOR KARLSTADT: This is incredible!

MARTIN LUTHER   (*When he starts to take hold of the
door, it falls toward him. One sees a room with a bed, two
tall lighted candles. A monk is inside, reading a book*): O
Lord Jesus, Saviour of the World, help us!

THE MONK   (*In the doorway*): Who disturbs the
silence of death? . . . So, it is you, doctor?

MARTIN LUTHER: What has happened? What has happened?

THE MONK: You mean you don't know?

MARTIN LUTHER: Don't know what?

THE MONK: Your friend Alexius is lying dead in
here. . . .

MARTIN LUTHER: Dead?

THE MONK: Yes—murdered!—Led astray, enticed by
evil companions! He was one of *your* friends, wasn't he,
doctor?

MARTIN LUTHER: Murdered? . . .

THE MONK: Whether by his own hand or by someone
else, we don't know. . . . Come inside and say a prayer for
your friend now. . . . He will need it—and so will you!

MARTIN LUTHER: No—I couldn't look at him! I can't

bear seeing blood! And I feel no guilt for what has happened!

THE MONK: No? . . . I have been told you pushed aside a despairing man yesterday. . . .

MARTIN LUTHER: Yes—that I did, alas! And my sin is too great to be forgiven me!

KARLSTADT: Come, let us leave this place, Martin! Come!

MARTIN LUTHER: How frightful, how horrible! Poor Alexius!

THE MONK: The voice of thy brother's blood crieth unto thee from the ground. . . .

KARLSTADT: Be quiet, monk! Come along, Martin! Let us leave this place!

MARTIN LUTHER: Where shall I go from Your spirit, where shall I flee from Your presence, Lord . . . Almighty God in Heaven. . . ?

THE MONK: Indeed!—"I have seen the wicked in great power, and spreading himself like a green bay tree. Yet he passed away, and lo, he was not: yea, I sought him, but he could not be found."—

Yes—that's how it goes. . . .

(*Martin Luther and Doctor Karlstadt leave.*)

End of Scene Two

Scene III

Luther's own home.
A table, set with wine, flowers and lights.
Several musical instruments lie on the table also.
Lucas Cranach and Ulrich von Hutten are seen admiring the table arrangement.

LUCAS CRANACH: This looks truly festive! Do you know the purpose of this celebration, Von Hutten?

ULRICH VON HUTTEN: No, Cranach, I don't. Doctor Luther and I have only met casually at the library, and I am a little astonished to find myself invited.

LUCAS CRANACH: Our good Martin loves song and laughter. He has been quite depressed the last few days, especially after that murder. . . . Alexius was a friend of his as you know. . . . I suppose he wants to dispel his grief in the company of friends. . . . And he is doing right in that.

ULRICH VON HUTTEN: I would do the same. . . .

SPALATIN (*Enters*): Look who are here! Two friends— Cranach and Von Hutten!—But where is our host?

LUCAS CRANACH: I ask you the same—you ought to know, Spalatin. . . .

SPALATIN: No, I don't. The Elector has had his eye on Doctor Martin—he wants to have him appointed a professor. . . . But this latest incident has to quiet down first. . . .

LUCAS CRANACH: Yes, it's been unpleasant for Luther, and yet he is not implicated in it in any way.

SPALATIN: No, that's true, but he has to learn to choose his companions. . . .

LUCAS CRANACH: He'll never learn that! His rashness plays many a prank on him. He is a wonderful man, and he'll survive this, too, without doubt.—See—see how he understands to arrange things. . . . It resembles a painting!
(*Doctor Karlstadt enters*)

LUCAS CRANACH: Karlstadt! The secretive one looks even more secretive than usual! Where have you the master of the house, our host?

KARLSTADT: Our host sends a greeting to his guests and asks them to commence the celebration. He himself will be here a little later.

LUCAS CRANACH: Has anything happened? I mean—besides that unfortunate incident?

KARLSTADT: I don't know. . . . Martin has been brooding lately. . . . And I don't know what might have happened last night.

ULRICH VON HUTTEN: He was on his way to his parents at Mansfeld—but a storm broke out and he turned back.

KARLSTADT: Yes, it was frightful weather last night . . . the thunder and lightning were pretty bad, I understand. . . .

LUCAS CRANACH: Yes, I could hear it thundering west of here. . . . But just what is it you are keeping from us, Karlstadt?

KARLSTADT: Well, Martin! He hears so much and sees so much—as I said, he is always brooding. . . .

LUCAS CRANACH: H'm!

KARLSTADT: He raved about the lightning striking close by him, and that he was knocked down—and then he heard someone speak to him, of course. . . . But now—let us sit down at table, good sirs, and I shall, with your permission, and at the request of our host, act as *rex bibendi* and do the honors.   (*They all seat themselves.*)

(*Hieronymos Schurff and Amsdorff enter.*)

KARLSTADT: You late-comers, step forward! Hieronymos Schurff—a judge who has never imposed the death penalty on anyone; Amsdorff, less known, who will attain fame in the future!

(*He knocks on the table after the servant has filled the glasses.*)

Estisne preparati?

ALL: *Sumus!*

KARLSTADT: *In honorem hospitis absentis, doctoris Martini Lutheri! Semel, bis.* . . .

ALL: *Ter!*   (*They empty their glasses.*)

LUCAS CRANACH: A song! Von Hutten will sing for us!

ALL: Yes, a song!

ULRICH VON HUTTEN: I can't sing—my throat is out of
order—but I shall recite a verse or two if Lucas will accompany me on his lute.

LUCAS CRANACH: Certainly. What are you going to
recite?

ULRICH VON HUTTEN: The Niebelungen ditty!

LUCAS CRANACH (*Strums an introduction*): I am
ready!

(*Doctor Johannes slides softly into the room. He sits down.*)

ULRICH VON HUTTEN   (*Recites*): My first young love, my
        very first, I to a woman gave;
she was a southern, torrid belle, and I became her slave,
her weakness I was given in return for strength she took—
and penitent and cankered I the house of joy forsook. . . .

Now I am doomed to celibacy until my dying day,
and Mercury must make amends where Venus brought
        decay;
and when my body has been purged by sulphur and by fast,
upon my staff I'll totter with my lute unto the last. . . .

You murderous black angel—you came from rotten Rome,
emerging from the dust and dirt with heretic
        heathendom. . . .
Now like a holocaust the German lands you're sweeping—
In Saxony and Thuringia joy's turned to grief and weeping.

Wake up, you Germans, all of you! Your youth is in a snare
of foreign pestilence and plague, I warn you to beware! . . .
And yet—the oak of Germany shall guard its precious home,
grow green, once rid its rotten root—the root that is called
        Rome!

ALL: Hew off the rotten root! That rotten root is Rome!

(*Doctor Johannes rises and bows to Ulrich von Hutten.*)

KARLSTADT: Lift your beakers in a toast to Von Hutten!

ALL: Ulrich von Hutten!!

(*Other Guests enter and seat themselves.*)

LUCAS CRANACH: This almost reminds me of a funeral —all are drinking—all but our host. . . .

KARLSTADT: He is absent for good cause!

MARTIN LUTHER   (*Enters*): This is a burial ceremony, my good friends!

ALL: Luther!   (*They rise.*)

MARTIN LUTHER   (*Seats himself at one end of the table*): Today Doctor Luther ceases to exist . . . for he leaves this world and its pleasures this very night—and, for reasons that cannot be told in just a few words, he is entering the Augustinian monastery here.

ALL: Oh no!

MARTIN LUTHER: That is my decision—and it cannot be changed!

LUCAS CRANACH: This is murder!

ULRICH VON HUTTEN: It is suicide! Don't do it! I was in the monastery at Fulda for five years, and I fled from that den of Sodom. Don't do it!

MARTIN LUTHER: It is an *ex–voto*, a promise to God given in the face of death, and in spiritual distress. . . .

LUCAS CRANACH: You can be freed from that vow. . . .

SPALATIN: The Elector can arrange that. . . .

MARTIN LUTHER: No, my friends, only I can do that— by redeeming my pledge. . . .

KARLSTADT: Luther is right.

MARTIN LUTHER: And it is for this reason, my noble friends and benefactors, that I have asked you to come here

that I may take leave of you.   (*He raises his beaker.*)
My childhood was no bed of roses—neither was my youth.
If that is what life has to offer, I relinquish it gladly. I hold
this cup in my hand, but I shall not drink of it. I pour it
out, an offering to your health and good fortune, an offering
of thanks for your friendship. . . . And I break this glass as
I shall now break with life and its frailties, its fleeting happiness. . . .   (*He breakes the glass.*)
Farewell, my friends . . . never again shall we meet—tomorrow Doctor Martin will be buried—and the day after I
shall exist only as Brother Augustine.

ALL: No! No!

SPALATIN: You have made up your mind—irrevocably?

MARTIN LUTHER: Irrevocably! Live happily, do not
forget me, and let love rule among you always. . . .
                                    (*He leaves.*)

ULRICH VON HUTTEN: You are leaving us, Augustine—
but Martin Luther will return!

LUCAS CRANACH: What is the meaning of all this?
What a sad end to such a brilliant beginning!

SPALATIN: I believe in the resurrection of the dead. . . .

ULRICH VON HUTTEN: He goes to hide himself in a
monastery—yet I vow that in ten years all cloisters and
monasteries will be closed!

DOCTOR JOHANNES   (*In a weak but convincing voice*):
My dear sirs, our friend Martin has a better conception of
siege and attack than we have. He enters the fortress and
opens the gates from within. Let us accompany him on his
way!

ALL: Let us do that! . . . . . .

End of Act Two

Act III

Scene I

The Augustinian monastery at Erfurt.
Two monks are seated by the fireplace. They are cracking
nuts.

(*Martin Luther enters with a broom and a sack.*)

FIRST MONK: Well, Augustine, my lad, did you sweep
the street?

MARTIN LUTHER: It's done.

SECOND MONK: Well, have you anything in the sack
that is good?

MARTIN LUTHER: I have something in it, but I don't
know what it is.

FIRST MONK (*Examines the contents of the sack*):
You are well liked by all the servant maids in the town,
aren't you? Whenever you go begging, you always bring
back something good to eat.

MARTIN LUTHER: Have you no shame?

SECOND MONK: Do you want to be disciplined again,
do you?

(*Martin Luther makes the sign of the cross over his mouth*
and is heard mumbling something.)

FIRST MONK: The tongue is a minor corporeal part,
        but it can bring sense to both mind and heart.

MARTIN LUTHER (*Falls on his knees*): Forgive me,
father!

SECOND MONK: I forgive you—but don't sin hereafter.
Obedience is first and foremost among the rules!—Let me see

now if you have learned to obey! Sit up, and I'll let you taste something good if you open your mouth! . . . One, two, three!

(*Martin Luther is silent; he does not move.*)

SECOND MONK: Sit up!

MARTIN LUTHER: No!

SECOND MONK: *Pax in pace!* You know what that is, don't you—down in the cellar?—Sit up!

MARTIN LUTHER: No!

FIRST MONK: Perjurer! You have vowed to obey the monastic rules and regulations, and you break your vow!

MARTIN LUTHER: I have lost the power of speech! It seems to me I have landed in hell and that you are demons! But perhaps I have deserved it all! Oh, Lord, how long will you so completely forget me?

SECOND MONK: You had better behave, Augustine, or you will be going to bed without supper. . . .

FIRST MONK: To think that we who know nothing have been assigned a learned doctor of laws to sweep the street for us! A genuine scholar who knows Latin and Greek. . . .

SECOND MONK: And then he has the audacity to complain that the other doctors don't speak to him!—If you put your light under a bushel measure, it will go out, of course. . . .

FIRST MONK: Tell me, Augustine,—I think it's so amusing to have to call him Augustine—have you read The Confessions of St. Augustine? It has some pretty juicy morsels in it. . . .

MARTIN LUTHER: I have read St. Augustine. . . .

FIRST MONK: He was quite a bright lad in his youth!

MARTIN LUTHER: When you speak of the founder of our holy order, speak with respect, or I'll report you to the Chapter!

SECOND MONK: Just listen to him!

THIRD MONK   (*Enters from the right*): Father Nicodemus—is it permissible to loan out the writings of Johann
Huss from the library?

FIRST MONK: Huss? Huss in hell!—Well, if you really
mean Huss—then let them read—it's nothing but drivel!
Who is it who wants it?

THIRD MONK: It's that crazy Doctor Johannes. . . .

FIRST MONK: You don't say! Is he here? Let's see what
he looks like!

(*He rises and goes toward the door with the two other
monks.*)

SECOND MONK: He is the one who is said to have sold
his soul to the devil! I want to take a look at him!

THIRD MONK: He already has the book—and the Elector himself had him sign for it. What do you think of that?

FIRST MONK: The Elector of Saxony? Are you out of
your mind?   (*He goes out, right, with the other monks.*)
(*Martin Luther is alone. He stands with his arms folded
across his chest, in prayer.*)
(*Doctor Johannes enters from the left, a book in his hand.*)

MARTIN LUTHER: *Vade retro, Satanas!*

DOCTOR JOHANNES: I once placed a book in your
hand, Doctor Luther, and that book became to you a shining light!—Read now in this one—just a few lines. . . .

MARTIN LUTHER: I do not wish to!

(*Doctor Johannes opens the book and holds it before him.*)

MARTIN LUTHER   (*Reads for a moment or two*): No!

DOCTOR JOHANNES: Just a line or two more!

MARTIN LUTHER: Yes, it is so—it is true. . . . But Huss
is a heretic!   (*He reads.*)
I wish I had never seen this book! Take it away! . . . Eternal, all-merciful God in Heaven! . . . Have we reached the
stage that the lie acts with the power of truth, and the truth

with that of the lie? . . . I believe I am a heretic—and therefore a damned and doomed soul! I am accursed—damned—
and God has cast me out, turned his back upon me . . . or
is he sleeping? Are you asleep, O Lord, or are you playing
a game with us? Go, Satan, and take your book with you—or
I'll slay you at the altar like a priest of Baal! Go!

DOCTOR JOHANNES: May peace be with you, Martin!
(*He leaves.*)
(*Martin Luther is alone, his arms folded in prayerful
meditation.*)

STAUPITZ   (*Enters*): Well, my son, how is your spirit
now?

MARTIN LUTHER: Unutterably broken!

STAUPITZ: *Contritio animi*—the crushing of the spirit—
is a good thing to go through. . . . But *conscientia scrupu-
losa*—or, a vain, petty conscience—that is arrogance!

MARTIN LUTHER: I am humble in spirit. . . .

STAUPITZ: No, you are not. You are the most arrogant
human being I have ever met. You wish to be perfect like
God and torture yourself with trivialities. . . . You go to
confession every day—but have nothing to confess. . . .

MARTIN LUTHER: My misdeeds are too great to be
forgiven.

STAUPITZ: Shame on you! Cannot God give you forgiveness for everything—even the trifling little trespasses of
an Augustine?

MARTIN LUTHER: They are not trifling. . . .

STAUPITZ: Because you want to see everything about
you magnified!

MARTIN LUTHER: God is angry with me!

STAUPITZ: God is good! And so he tests you compassionately! And that is a grace!

MARTIN LUTHER: It is not a punishment, then?

STAUPITZ: You have not committed any crimes, have you?

MARTIN LUTHER: Not in the usual sense. . . .

STAUPITZ: Then stop putting plasters on your soul. . . . You keep plastering it, Augustine!—Use surgery instead!—Are you otherwise content with your life in the monastery?

(*Martin Luther is silent.*)

STAUPITZ: No, you are not. And neither am I. That is why I have sought some activity outside the confines of the monastery. I am teaching at the university. Would you like to do the same?

MARTIN LUTHER: What would I teach?

STAUPITZ: Philosophy, and the languages of the ancients.

MARTIN LUTHER: Philosophy is a pagan cult. . . .

STAUPITZ: . . . which we shall now baptize! And the languages of old shall serve us—not be our masters!

MARTIN LUTHER: I dislike them!

STAUPITZ: That's a mistake! The Bible is written in the languages of the Hebrews and the Greeks—they are therefore sacred languages. . . . Make no mistake about that!—However, the Elector summons you to become a professor at the university—and when *he* summons, you obey!

MARTIN LUTHER: I can't serve two masters!

STAUPITZ: Can't you do what we others can do? We serve both the emperor and the pope, and the Elector too, for that matter. You are a great talker—but you shall become an orator. . . . Tell me, my son, has it ever occurred to you that you may have a special calling?

MARTIN LUTHER: Yes—at times! There are times when I am stirred by a consciousness of being imbued with a power so great that I feel as if I could stay the river Rhine in its course—or carry away the Black Forest. . . .

STAUPITZ: Now I shall tell you something—but don't

let it turn your head! All have had their eyes on you for
some time!—Nobody knows exactly why—for you have
accomplished nothing as yet. . . . But we all expect something of you—something great!

MARTIN LUTHER: Of a poor wretch like me?

STAUPITZ: Yes—of you—as was the fate of the poor
little Samuel!

MARTIN LUTHER: Samuel?—Why, that's exactly what
I read in the Elector's library! Samuel!

STAUPITZ: Yes!

MARTIN LUTHER: That was it, then? That was it!—
"Here we have need of a Samuel—but where can he be
found?"

STAUPITZ: Here he is!

MARTIN LUTHER   (*Kneels*): Yes and amen—so be it!

STAUPITZ: But before you enter upon your duties as
a teacher, you must carry out a task that in itself is a test!

MARTIN LUTHER   (*With his eyes toward heaven*):
Speak, O Lord, your servant hears you!

STAUPITZ: You are to bring a missive to the Holy
Father in Rome. . . .

MARTIN LUTHER: To Rome? I am to see the Holy
City? . . . The dream of my childhood—the hope and longing of my youth! . . .

STAUPITZ: Your dreams are beginning to come true....

MARTIN LUTHER: To Rome—I?

STAUPITZ: Yes . . . but keep your eyes open! See—
hear—and say nothing! When you return you may speak!
But only to me!—Remember that! . . . Thus: the door is
open! The bird may fly. . . . Fly out!

MARTIN LUTHER: Out! Out into the world! Then I am
not dead yet!

STAUPITZ: You?

End of Scene One

Scene II

Franz von Sickingen's Castle Ebernburg.
The printing shop. Typesetters and printers at work.
Ulrich von Hutten, Erasmus, and Reuchlin are seated at a
table. They are busy writing.

ULRICH VON HUTTEN (*Rises*): Get up and move about. . . . You will be decrepit if you sit still much longer. —Get up, Reuchlin!

REUCHLIN: Tell me, Ulrich—have you heard anything more from the Dominicans in Cologne?

ULRICH VON HUTTEN: Who wanted to burn you alive? Yes—can you imagine . . . they have ordered five hundred copies of our epistles against the Dark Men.

REUCHLIN: But that's ludicrous! What do you think it means?

ULRICH VON HUTTEN: It means that they are so stupid they don't understand satire. They have taken it literally!

ERASMUS (*With a smile*): I have never heard anything like it! Can the world have gone mad?

REUCHLIN: Don't trust them! You can't trust them! I know these saintly curs. . . . If we were not sitting here in safety with our friend Von Sickingen, then. . . .

ULRICH VON HUTTEN: Oh, but we have the emperor on our side, and Maximilian is planning to. . . .

ERASMUS: Planning what? You mean he plans to take away the pope's political power and put an end to these dissensions in Germany?

ULRICH VON HUTTEN: Yes—that's his idea! And that is the core of the whole matter! We have a legislature, a Court of Justice, and our own laws—but our legislation and our laws are constantly being crossed by the canonical laws and decretals of Rome! How can the cart go forward, I ask, if you harness an ox at each end? If the harness holds, all's well and good—but just now the cart is being strained and is about to go to pieces.

ERASMUS: It's amazing that we have come so far that the emperor is beginning to catch on to the pope. . . .

REUCHLIN: Herod and Pilate can become friends again once they find someone to crucify!

FRANZ VON SICKINGEN (*Enters with a letter*): Here you are plodding and writing, I see. . . . But now let us get together for a little talk, for I have much news for you!

ULRICH VON HUTTEN (*Stretching himself*): Let's hear, let's hear!

FRANZ VON SICKINGEN: Well—this is the way the land lies. . . . Your epistles are being read throughout the whole of Germany—from the Elbe to the Rhine! And everybody is chuckling!

ULRICH VON HUTTEN: Are they laughing? Then we are getting somewhere!

FRANZ VON SICKINGEN: The people are laughing at the monks—and now the Dominicans in Cologne have at last discovered the prank, and they are raging! . . . See— here you see their warning to you!

REUCHLIN: Well, I'll be. . . .

ERASMUS: What can they do to us here at Ebernburg?

ULRICH VON HUTTEN: You know the dogs, Reuchlin. . . . They are bird dogs. . . . They don't bark—but they can crawl on their bellies.

REUCHLIN: A Dominican can pass through locked doors, crawl in the gutter, or through a privy. One might almost say he scents his way to his prey!

FRANZ VON SICKINGEN (*Pointing to the printers and typesetters*): You know all these men, Ulrich?

ULRICH VON HUTTEN: Most of them—not all.

FRANZ VON SICKINGEN: Be careful!—And now I'll give you some more news. . . . That Satan's archbishop in Mainz has sent out a Dominican, an immoral swine who goes by the name of Diezel or Tezel to sell indulgences. And the blackguard has even had printed a regular price list for these indulgences. For instance, he charges—if paid in cash, or *contantibus in manibus,* fifty ducats for polygamy, nine for stealing from the Church, or for swearing falsely, eight for murder, and two for witchcraft or magic.

ULRICH VON HUTTEN: What a swine! How much does he charge for simple adultery?

FRANZ VON SICKINGEN: He makes no mention of that, for he himself has been caught twice at that. But when they put him in a sack and tried to drown him in the Danube, the archbishop of Mainz interceded, and he was given mercy.

ERASMUS: Why, that's about the worst I have heard.

REUCHLIN: But the very stupidity of it is what will help us. . . .

ULRICH VON HUTTEN: It's unbelievable what they do to destroy themselves!

FRANZ VON SICKINGEN: Well—if the apple isn't ripe now—then it is rotten!

ULRICH VON HUTTEN: And now—let us waste no time but feed the dainty little morsel I have here in the box, to the presses!—Let's wait with the new edition of the epistles! —Throw in the circular in the press!—And then let everybody get busy with the typesetting. . . . Let's start setting it up!—First, the presses and the forms!

(*He takes off his armor and goes over to the press.*) Oiler! Get busy!

FRANZ VON SICKINGEN: And, can you imagine, that Tezel is traveling round with his two sons!

REUCHLIN: What a horrible beast!

ERASMUS: Yes—what's happened to the celibacy? They ought to castrate them!

FRANZ VON SICKINGEN: You know that Doctor Luther —who went into a monastery. . . . They say he is in Rome now. . . .

ERASMUS: It's amazing how much that man is being spoken of. . . .

REUCHLIN: Has he ever written anything?

ERASMUS: No—but some people attain renown for no reason whatever.

ULRICH VON HUTTEN (*While working the press, recites*): Start the press! Come on, align!

CHORUS: Yes, let it go!

ULRICH VON HUTTEN: Let the precious grape give wine!

CHORUS: Let us press it, let it flow!

ULRICH VON HUTTEN: Let us write in black and white!

CHORUS: Oh, come on there!

ULRICH VON HUTTEN: Let us give it to them right!

CHORUS: So beware!

ULRICH VON HUTTEN: What in the name of Jerusalem's shoemaker is this? It won't print!—The press is out of order! It's dripping with oil! Who is responsible for this? Who?—We have a traitor among us!—Who is he? Can it be the oiler?—You turn pale, you satan!—Off with your cap! His pate is shaved! Come here, Reuchlin, and have a sniff at him! See if you can tell whether he is a Dominican. . . .

REUCHLIN (*Steps forward and makes believe he is smelling him*): He smells of dog piss. He is a Dominican!

ULRICH VON HUTTEN: Out through the window with him! Out! . . . All men on deck! Six floors' handicap to eternity! And the grave is wet! Put out that hell fire! . . . Let us press it, let it flow! Oh, come on there! Yes, let it go!

(*The Oiler is hoisted out through the window.*)

ULRICH VON HUTTEN (*Gazes out of the window after him*): He didn't fall in the moat! He landed squarely across a Spanish cavalryman—so there is no danger he'll be having any children. . . .

ERASMUS: With his Spanish caparison on—no!

ULRICH VON HUTTEN: We certainly can be glad we got rid of that one!

FRANZ VON SICKINGEN: And now they will try to storm the castle, of course!

ULRICH VON HUTTEN: Then let us get out while there is time! But where—where shall we go? Shall we go to Wittenberg, friends? There is excitement, there. . . .

FRANZ VON SICKINGEN: I am staying, definitely, for that diabolic archbishop is bound to be coming here after what has happened!

ERASMUS: I am not budging!

REUCHLIN: He provides us with such wonderful food here—our friend Franz—that I hold fast here—like the rat caught in the cheese.

ULRICH VON HUTTEN: Well—then I shall go to Wittenberg alone—for there I have both printing press and friends. . . . And, I want to meet that scoundrel Tezel with whom I have a goose to pluck—he'll be there. Hail to you, noble Sickingen—knight without reproach! My hand, for the hospitality you have shown me! My foot is at your disposal, too, at all times—should you be in need of someone able to kick; my pen also, when your sword fails to bite; and my lute whenever you wish a sorrow eased!   (*He leaves.*)

(*At the door he turns, saluting them with*): *Hic,* Waiblings!

End of Scene Two

Scene III

A room in the Elector of Saxony's castle.
On the wall is seen a fresco painting of Laocoön.
The Elector and Spalatin.

THE ELECTOR: Is it the monk Augustine who is waiting outside?

SPALATIN: Yes, it is he, just returned from Rome.

THE ELECTOR: He has to wait!—So he is back already? . . . Yes—you see, my good Spalatin, this tradesman in indulgences, this Tezel, is a reprehensible scoundrel, once sentenced to be drowned. The Archbishop of Magdeburg, who is the Elector of Mainz, and Albrecht of Brandenburg pleaded to have the sentence revoked—yet I was given the blame for it. What have I to say in spiritual matters? I haven't the slightest influence in ecclesiastical affairs—and that is what is so unfortunate for this German land of ours. I don't possess the power to exile him—I can't put a stop to his infamous trade in indulgences. All I can do is to have him preached against. But he is so clever with his big mouth that he can outtalk anybody. Consequently I am helpless—don't know what to do. . . .

SPALATIN: Your Grace—I have at my disposal the loudest mouth in all Germany. . . .

THE ELECTOR: You mean the monk Augustine, or Doctor Luther as he was called before. . . . Let me take a look at this remarkable bird whom everybody is talking about.

SPALATIN: His language is a little untamed, so Your Grace will. . . .

THE ELECTOR: That doesn't matter at all—on the contrary. . . . Let him come in!

(*Spalatin goes out and returns with Martin Luther.*)

THE ELECTOR: You were a doctor of jurisprudence and your name was Luther, wasn't it?

MARTIN LUTHER: That is correct!

THE ELECTOR: You became a monk in order to study the monastic life, didn't you?

MARTIN LUTHER: No, for other reasons. . . .

THE ELECTOR: You have been in Rome. . . . How did you find it there?

MARTIN LUTHER: I can't tell you.

THE ELECTOR: Was it that bad?

MARTIN LUTHER: It was indescribable!

THE ELECTOR: Tell me!

MARTIN LUTHER: I can't. My tongue, my teeth, my gums refuse me—and if I were to wash my eyes and ears in the salt water of the sea, they would never be clean of all the filth and excrement I saw and heard there. . . . There they hold a court more pagan than in the times of Nero, Caligula, and Domitian. That might be overlooked—but for the fact that they believe in nothing. They are even more of infidels than the Turks, the Moors, and the Aztecs. The priests make a mockery of the very holiest—and within the walls of Rome nothing is left of Christianity. . . .

THE ELECTOR: Is it really that bad?

MARTIN LUTHER: It is.

THE ELECTOR: Augustine! You are appointed a professor in Wittenberg! But first you are to inspect the monasteries! You are familiar with the monasteries, aren't you?

MARTIN LUTHER: They are the only whorehouses and drinking places I know!

THE ELECTOR: At the same time you shall preach against that dealer in indulgences, Tezel.

MARTIN LUTHER: Six months ago I would have said

no. . . . But now I say yes and amen—and God bless Your Grace!

THE ELECTOR: Well—go first and see Staupitz. He will give you your instructions.

(*Martin Luther casts a glance at the fresco painting of the Laocoön.*)

THE ELECTOR: You are looking at the priest there. . . . Beware of the snake pit!—And remember one thing—do not touch my relics!

MARTIN LUTHER: I had thought I'd start with them!

THE ELECTOR: Spalatin! See the monk out! And tell him all he needs to know!

End of Scene Three

Scene IV

Before the portal of the castle chapel in Wittenberg. Organ music is heard from within.
Doctor Karlstadt and Melanchthon enter.

KARLSTADT: Brother Melanchthon, I have summoned you because I need help and advice.

MELANCHTHON: Do not overestimate me—but tell me what burdens your heart.

KARLSTADT: Today, All Saints' Day, our friend Luther has asked his comrades to gather here at the entrance of this church on the stroke of six. For what purpose he didn't say. . . . But, after finishing his visitation to the monasteries, he has been excessively agitated, almost raging. In his capacity as priest he has had occasion to hear confessions. A few days ago he told me of the following incident. A person who had committed perjury came to Luther to confess his sin. Luther told him to do penance for it, and promised him absolution if he repented and mended his ways. And can you imagine what he answered? The perjurer declared he was neither going to do penance nor mend his ways, for he had bought and paid for the right to commit perjury.

MELANCHTHON: That's the indulgence racket. . . .

KARLSTADT: Yes, that's the pope and his agent Tezel.

MELANCHTHON: It's abominable, insufferable!

KARLSTADT: Luther feels the same way. He is beyond himself, and I fear he may commit some imprudent act. One can never tell what he may have in mind!

MELANCHTHON: What do you suggest that we do, Karlstadt? As far as I can see, there is nothing we *can* do.

KARLSTADT: If you think so—then let us wait. . . .

MELANCHTHON: We have waited a long time, and all of us are still waiting. . . . Well—let us be patient and wait a while longer!

KARLSTADT: Yes—until six o'clock—but no longer!

MELANCHTHON: What's going on inside—in the chapel?

KARLSTADT: A mass is being held in connection with a display of the relics. The Elector has deposited the nineteen thousand relics he has collected, in his new church.

MELANCHTHON: The devout Elector!

(*They walk to and fro.*)
(*Lucas Cranach and Hans Sachs enter.*)

LUCAS CRANACH: You haven't sung for some years now, friend Sachs, have you?

HANS SACHS: No, the twilight has set in—and I have to have sunshine!—What is to take place here tonight, and why have we been summoned?

LUCAS CRANACH: I can't help feeling that from now on we may expect nothing more from our good Luther after he took up the monastic life. Nonetheless I would like to see him and talk to him.—We'll wait until six, won't we?

HANS SACHS: I am anxious to see that man!
   (*Again they start walking back and forth.*)
   DOCTOR JOHANNES   (*Enters with Amsdorff*): This is
a cathedral, a Christian church—but in Rome they are build-
ing pagan temples. Even St. Peter's which is now being
built, is a conglomeration of basilica and Pantheon. Rome
has no cathedral.
   AMSDORFF: And it is to complete St. Peter's that Tezel
is going around collecting money?
   DOCTOR JOHANNES: Yes, Christendom pays for its sins,
pays tribute to the pagans! The pope collects ancient Roman manuscripts—he recently paid several hundred ducats
for a book by Livius—but for the Bible he doesn't give two
farthings.
   AMSDORFF: Where does this new paganism come
from?
   DOCTOR JOHANNES: Some say from Constantinople,
after the Turks had driven the Greeks over into Rome. . . .
   AMSDORFF: Where will it end? Christianity is in
danger!
   DOCTOR JOHANNES: Oh no!—There is a purpose in
everything!   (*They walk to and fro.*)
   (*Ulrich von Hutten and Schurff enter.*)
   ULRICH VON HUTTEN: The dice has been cast and the
six turned up!—But what are people waiting for here?
   SCHURFF: For Martin Luther. . . .
   ULRICH VON HUTTEN: People have been waiting for
him for a long time! He has been clucking enough for the
egg—but he has never produced one!
   SCHURFF: He will soon—and it won't be just wind!
   ULRICH VON HUTTEN: The sledging is hard here at
the entrance, and brother Martin has been dragging his
load much too long across rocks and stones.
   (*Father Luther and Mother Luther enter.*)

FATHER LUTHER: This, I suppose, is the castle church?

MOTHER LUTHER: Yes, that's what they say.

FATHER LUTHER: If I could only speak with him— just one word. . . .

MOTHER LUTHER: But don't be too hard on him—you know what a quick temper he has. Why don't you let me speak instead?

FATHER LUTHER: No, I want to do it myself. I am in such a rage, I feel like striking him down. . . .

(*The clock in the church strikes six times.—All gather near the portal in tense anticipation of what is to come.*)

ULRICH VON HUTTEN: Isn't he coming?

SCHURFF: He will be here.

LUCAS CRANACH: What do you think it all means?

HANS SACHS: They look so disturbed. . . .

MELANCTHON: May God help us! What is to happen?

KARLSTADT: Amen, amen. . . . It shall so be!

HANS SACHS: Here he comes! Look at him! Yes, it is he—coming in the name of the Lord! It is he!

                         (*Martin Luther enters.*)

MOTHER LUTHER (*Goes toward him*): My son, your father and I have been seeking you. . . .

MARTIN LUTHER: Woman, what have I with you to do?   (*Father Luther steps forward.*)

MARTIN LUTHER: My ways are not your ways. . . .

(*He goes up to the portal. Then he produces a hammer, nails and a placard, which he attaches with three nails. At the first sound of the hammer, the organ becomes silent.*) In the name of the Holy Trinity—The Father, The Son, and the Holy Ghost! Amen!

ULRICH VON HUTTEN (*Advances to the portal and reads*): Ninety-five theses against the indulgences!

MARTIN LUTHER: Here are the theses! My defense of them will be heard from the pulpit . . . not in the street!

(*Spalatin and Staupitz enter, holding placards.*)

SPALATIN: Peace, Martin!

STAUPITZ: Peace!

MARTIN LUTHER: I have not come to bring peace without conflict! Fire and sword, death and destruction! Almighty, living God, stand by me and protect me, then I shall fear neither the pope in Rome nor the demons in Hell!

(*He leaves.*)

HANS SACHS: Now the sun has risen over Germany once more! Now we can sing again—shall sing new songs. New songs, Von Hutten! And you, Cranach—you shall paint a new picture of our land!

(*All clasp each others' hands in jubilation.*)

End of Scene Four

Scene V

The greenhouse in the Peutingers' garden, with a statue of Laocoön, at Augsburg.
The Dominican from Sickingen's castle and The Monk from Alexius' deathbed are seen in conversation.

THE DOMINICAN: I wish I had died when they threw me into the ditch at Sickingen's castle!

THE MONK: I can well understand that. . . . I don't believe in miracles, but that you escaped with your life—*that is* a miracle!

THE DOMINICAN: When I think that this Von Hutten —who is the author of that scurrilous pamphlet, that blasphemous lampoon of the monks . . . when I think that this rotten knave was dubbed a knight yesterday by Emperor Maximilian and today was made poet laureate and crowned with a laurel wreath by the hand of the marvelously beautiful Constantia von Peutinger, then I want to die!

THE MONK: I don't care about all this you say about Von Hutten—but that a whoremonger like this Luther is going to inspect the monasteries—why, that's like having a goat tend your garden . . . it's the height of presumption and impudence! It's shameless!

THE DOMINICAN: Yes, Luther. . . . I wonder how far Cajetanus has come with him up there in the consistory today?

THE MONK: The papal legate has done everything but make away with the louse. Still, although he has been trampled flat, there is life in him. He refuses to take back a single thing! What are you going to do with anyone like that?

THE DOMINICAN: Murder him!

THE MONK: Yes—that's what should be done to him! But he has spread his seeds so terrifically that the whole of Germany is sprouting with his thistles.

THE DOMINICAN: You don't mean it?

THE MONK: There is not one in a hundred on our side today.—This Lutheranism is raging like the *morbus Gallicus*. . . .

THE DOMINICAN: As regards *morbus Gallicus*—they say that Von Hutten is courting Constantia Peutinger. . . . Have you heard that?

THE MONK: Yes, that's what they say. . . .

THE DOMINICAN: Then she can't know that he is infected. . . .

THE MONK: She couldn't! If she did, she wouldn't have him.

THE DOMINICAN: Well, then she will be told! Have you noticed that he always wears gloves?

THE MONK: Yes, why does he?

THE DOMINICAN: His hands have become infected, of course. She'll find that out, too.

THE MONK: She'll never believe it! Don't you know anything about women? When they are in love, they will kiss anything—a drowned cat or a dog with rabies.

THE DOMINICAN: Then I'll go to see old man Peutinger, her father. . . . And I won't waste any time. . . .

THE MONK: Aren't you going to listen to the disputation first?

THE DOMINICAN: No, I am not interested in theology.

THE MONK: I would like to exchange a few blows with that big-mouthed fellow. Believe it or not, I know how to handle myself. . . .

THE DOMINICAN: I am going to Peutinger—this minute—to squash Von Hutten for good. I leave it to you to do the same to Luther. . . . *Suum cuique!*

THE MONK: But hurry before it is too late!

THE DOMINICAN: Now, Von Hutten, you are going to get a thorn in your flesh!   (*He leaves.*)

THE MONK (*Alone*): Well, well. . . .

(*Martin Luther enters. He is busy writing something in a book.*)

THE MONK (*Approaches Luther*): Dear Brother Augustine. . . .

MARTIN LUTHER: Quiet!

THE MONK: Brother deputy inspector. . . .

MARTIN LUTHER: Keep your mouth shut!

THE MONK: Is it true that you have recanted? That you have uttered the six little letters *revoco* on bended knees—I—take—it—back, as the farmer said when he had committed perjury?

MARTIN LUTHER: That's a lie, you liar!—Yes—he who lies is a liar! But you have a face that tells no lie: it's like a slate that has been spat upon, and where all the vices, even the most secret, can be plainly read. I have visited your monastery, and so I know your bunk, your table, your wash bowl, your cups, and decanter. . . .

(*The Monk tries vainly to get a chance to speak.*)

MARTIN LUTHER: . . . If I were to inspect your throat, it would be with a broom used for excrement. . . . The ooze of liquor in you is strong enough to make six farmers reeling drunk if they kissed you on the mouth. . . . Your nose is red as a bowl of berries and shines like a lantern, bright enough to pick earthworms by. . . . Your eyes resemble goose lard—and your ears would make fertile soil for a whole bucket of cowpeas. . . . You have the audacity to touch the holiest of the holy with your hands that have not been near water for well-nigh a year . . . and with your filthy snout you have kissed God's altar! . . . Yes—I met you once at the deathbed of my friend Alexius. I was very young and very stupid at that time—almost as stupid as you are. You made much ado about an unrighteous one who had made great strides in a wayward direction, and then suddenly was no more. Those words sank into me, a young student, as the word of God: with my tail between my legs, and ears closed, I crept into the hole. But had I known what I know now, I would never have put on the black robe or gone begging with the sack on my shoulder. Nevertheless, I thank you for all you have taught me. The apple lay close to the rod; but cunning is not wisdom, and the fraud and deception of the wicked and impious is not common sense, or wisdom. The dog returns to his vomit and a monk will poke in his own excrements! . . . What, I think you are choking, you beast?

(*The Monk crushed by rage, his back bent and his face livid, drags himself out.*)

MARTIN LUTHER: That's the way to tame a blackguard! (*There is a pause.*)

STAUPITZ   (*Enters from where the Monk just made his exit*): What did you do to the monk?

MARTIN LUTHER: Did I take his breath away?

STAUPITZ: I think you gave him apoplexy!

MARTIN LUTHER: Good! I can't be blamed for that!

STAUPITZ: Augustine . . . I can't go along with you any further!

MARTIN LUTHER: Can't you?

STAUPITZ: You have gone too far already!

MARTIN LUTHER: Are you abandoning me?

STAUPITZ: Yes!

MARTIN LUTHER: My father and my mother have abandoned me, too, but the Lord receives me!—What have I done?

STAUPITZ: You know what you have done!—You have called the pope Antichrist!

MARTIN LUTHER: As long as he *is* Antichrist, I shall call him that!

STAUPITZ: Are you going to argue with me, also?— No—I have only one thing to tell you. . . . From today on, you are freed from your monastic vow. . . .

MARTIN LUTHER: In brief, expelled!

STAUPITZ: If you will! Augustine does no longer exist. . . .

MARTIN LUTHER: Then I am again Martin Luther! Good! The robe was beginning to be a little constraining— it hampered me in my movements.

STAUPITZ: Are you thinking of soaring now?

MARTIN LUTHER: I shall take the wings of the rosy red dawn and fly to the source of the rising sun!

STAUPITZ: You have to fly alone then—no one wants to follow you!

MARTIN LUTHER: No one?—Has the Elector also . . . ?

STAUPITZ: Yes, the Elector has withdrawn because of your violent behavior. . . .

MARTIN LUTHER: He has deserted me? He, too! Very well! You are no longer my superior—therefore I can speak out! I shall say it in a few words. . . . For your benign and gracious protection in times of evil, I express my gratitude . . . for your faithlessnes to the Holy of the Holies, I curse you!

STAUPITZ: He curses me! O God, he curses his friend!
(*He weeps.*)

MARTIN LUTHER: Yes, I curse you!

STAUPITZ   (*Turns to go*): He curses his friend! May God forgive you! (*He leaves.*)

MARTIN LUTHER: He has already!   (*He is alone.*) Alone! . . . So much the better!   (*He starts to leave.*) Almighty, living God! Now You and I stand alone! Will you abandon me, too? I will not fail you!   (*He goes out.*) (*Ulrich von Hutten enters, wearing knight's armor and a laurel wreath on his head. He is accompanied by Constantia Peutinger.*)

ULRICH VON HUTTEN: This is the spot . . . here I shall read you my song. . . .

CONSTANTIA: . . . and your secret—you will tell it to me alone. . . .

ULRICH VON HUTTEN: If not to you—to whom? Is there anyone else but you? Does the world exist except through you? What am I without you? Only when I first saw you was I born, and I shall die when I no longer see you. . . .
Now I am ready to ascend the pyre . . . and I shall light it myself. . . .

CONSTANTIA: You speak in riddles. . . . You tell me you love me. . . . I answer: "Will you have me?"—You reply: "I want you—but I cannot take you!"—What is the rub? My

father, my mother, and myself—we all give our consent—yet
you say you cannot take me. . . .

ULRICH VON HUTTEN: The will of the gods—do you
know what that means?

CONSTANTIA: The gods! You are speaking of the old
Roman gods—as if you worshiped them. . . .

ULRICH VON HUTTEN: They have returned from their
exile, and we are honoring them today!

CONSTANTIA (*With a gesture toward the Laocoön*):
And this figure which you now see everywhere—who is he?

ULRICH VON HUTTEN: That figure has been given
many interpretations. The latest one is that Laocoön, Apollo's priest, was said to have married, and that he therefore
was slain by Apollo.

CONSTANTIA: Then Apollo never was in love. . . .

ULRICH VON HUTTEN: He never married. . . . He fell
in love with a maiden named Daphne—but, at the crucial
moment, she was transformed into—a laurel tree.—Constantia . . . the laurel was given me—but I shall never be given
you. . . .

CONSTANTIA: Again I ask you—sing your secret to me!

ULRICH VON HUTTEN: I cannot sing—but I shall recite
it—while I still have a voice. . . .

CONSTANTIA: Still, you say?

ULRICH VON HUTTEN: Yes . . . my voice is burning out,
just as the light in my eyes. Soon the journey in the dark is
commencing—and then—the silence. . . .   (*He recites.*)
At Spessartberg—
at Spessartberg, by Rhön,
Herr Wolkenstein—
Herr Wolkenstein von Schrön—
has built a fort with roots in rock,
from where he watches every city block,
and townsfolk as they flock

to say their prayers anon.

Herr Wolkenstein—
Herr Wolkenstein von Schrön—
has built his fortress by the Rhön. . . .
But higher still, on crest up high,
you see an ancient falcon fly . . .
they say he's kin to Satan sly. . . .
He lives up in the snow alone.

Herr Wolkenstein—
Herr Wolkenstein by Rhön—
beware, beware!
The rain, in torrents, whines and caws;
and by its nest the falcon claws. . . .
The brittle bridge of ice, it thaws—
it sways—it breaks—recedes—withdraws. . . .
The avalanche has now begun!

Herr Wolkenstein—
Herr Wolkenstein by Rhön—
his fort and he
are fast asleep in Rhön. . . .
He has a son who roams about,
a nobody, a seedy lout,
who never won a single bout—
and now his day is done!

At Spessartberg—
at Spessartberg and Rhön,
where oaks grow dense
upon the ridge of Rhön . . .
where neither mead nor wine you'll see,
by a ravine your bard will be—

to see the avalanche set free. . . .
Himself—decayed—a ruin wan!

CONSTANTIA   (*Is about to rush into his arms; he holds her back*):   You push me aside!

ULRICH VON HUTTEN;   Yes. . . .

CONSTANTIA: And yet you love me?

ULRICH VON HUTTEN: Yes! . . . And that is why we must part—for I am—your leprous brother!

(*Constantia gives a shriek.*)

PEUTINGER   (*Enters*):   Knight Ulrich von Hutten. . . .

ULRICH VON HUTTEN: Yes!

PEUTINGER: Our gracious Emperor and Lord has bestowed on you sword and spurs. But there is reason to doubt that you are a true noble, and—above all—that you are a defender of chastity and virginity.

ULRICH VON HUTTEN: Are you besmirching my shield and my honor, burgher! Take care!

PEUTINGER: So—you take that tone, you vagrant! . . . Constantia, this man is not worthy of you!

CONSTANTIA: He is, indeed, and he is a true knight and noble!

PEUTINGER: But you don't know what he. . . .

CONSTANTIA: Yes, I do know. . . . I know that he is suffering from a deadly malady . . . and that is why we have now taken leave of each other for life. . . .

PEUTINGER: Von Hutten—forgive me! Give me your hand!

ULRICH VON HUTTEN: No, I can't give you my hand—but I give you my heart—*that* is still clean. . . .

CONSTANTIA: Ulrich!

ULRICH VON HUTTEN: Constantia!

CONSTANTIA: Farewell—my forever beloved friend!

ULRICH VON HUTTEN: Farewell, forever beloved

friend! (*He departs.*)

PEUTINGER: Your saga of love, my child, was brief. . . .

CONSTANTIA: Brief as happiness! Only sorrow lingers on. . . .

PEUTINGER: Oh, that it must. . . .

(*Von Hutten and Constantia go toward the exit, followed by Peutinger. Peutinger remains, while Constantia goes out.*)

DOCTOR KARLSTADT (*Enters; to Peutinger*): Luther has fled!

PEUTINGER: Fled, you say? . . .

KARLSTADT: He has secretly left the city. . . .

PEUTINGER: Then all is lost!—Why should he destroy his own work?

KARLSTADT: And now we others have to take hold. . . .

PEUTINGER: Are you, Karlstadt, the man for that task?

KARLSTADT: I haven't always been—but now I am!

PEUTINGER: Are there others?

KARLSTADT: There are legions of us!—And now I am leaving for Leipzig to dispute with Eck! . . . When that is over, you will see what will happen!

PEUTINGER: Yes, we shall see. . . .

End of Scene Five

Scene VI

Doctor Johannes' laboratory in Leipzig.—

Doctor Johannes is seated at a table. He is speaking to someone not visible in a room to the left, rear. The door to this room stands open.

The moonlight illuminates Doctor Johannes' room; the other room is lit by a lamp and a smelting furnace.

DOCTOR JOHANNES: Answer me! What do you see?

THE VOICE: I see a white rose and a red eagle.

DOCTOR JOHANNES: The kingdoms of matter and spirit.

THE VOICE: Who is the ruler over matter?

DOCTOR JOHANNES: The Ghibelline. . . .

THE VOICE: Who is the ruler of the spirit?

DOCTOR JOHANNES: The Guelf. . . . What do you see now?

THE VOICE: The rose and the eagle engage in combat!

DOCTOR JOHANNES: Who is the victor?

THE VOICE: Neither! They seem to be equals in strength. . . .

DOCTOR JOHANNES: What do you see now?

THE VOICE: The white rose sprouts a red rose! Now the roses are battling each other. . . .

DOCTOR JOHANNES: Who is victorious?

THE VOICE: The red rose!

DOCTOR JOHANNES: That's Lancaster at Bosworth. . . . That's Henry!

THE VOICE: May I ask a question?

DOCTOR JOHANNES: Ask!

THE VOICE: What was in the beginning?

DOCTOR JOHANNES: All! All is all and in all! All serves all! —   (*There is a loud knock at a door on the right.*) Let's stop!

DOCTOR JOHANNES: Come in!

(*Doctor Karlstadt enters.*)

DOCTOR JOHANNES: You have asked if you might come and talk with me—like Nicodemus, in the middle of the night. Welcome!—What is on your mind?

KARLSTADT: I wish to know what the future holds. . . .

DOCTOR JOHANNES: That you can deduct from the present—that is, if you know how to calculate. . . . To find the unknown quantity when three known quantities are given, is easy.

KARLSTADT: Doctor Johannes, you have listened to our disputations here in Leipzig, haven't you?

DOCTOR JOHANNES: I have listened to you for seventeen days. . . .

KARLSTADT: Whom do you consider the victor?

DOCTOR JOHANNES: Neither one of you! You have both been equally crafty and cunning. The papists say that they hold the victory; the Lutherans vow that they came out best.

KARLSTADT: Is God on our side—or is he against us?

DOCTOR JOHANNES: He who is just, is neither for nor against; justice must be impartial.

KARLSTADT: Can papists lay claim to be right in any way whatsoever?

DOCTOR JOHANNES: Why, of course. Just as the temporal powers have their emperor, so the spiritual forces have their pope.—And the spiritual interests should come first, shouldn't they?—

KARLSTADT: But the pope's political power . . . ?

DOCTOR JOHANNES: What power exactly are you speaking of? The Archbishop of Rome has his diocese or prebend just like the rest of the bishops, so that's not worth discussing. The power of Leo X was not great enough to prevent him from being taken prisoner at Ravenna. . . .

KARLSTADT: I regret having had this discussion with you. . . .

DOCTOR JOHANNES: That's exactly what Luther said when I gave him Huss's writings to read. Yet he is now standing in the pulpit proclaiming himself a Hussite!—However, you have already been given justice, haven't you? Tezel has been repudiated and his trading in indulgences has been forbidden. The papal chamberlain Miltizt, Luther's fiercest enemy, has gone to the bottom of the Rhine after indulging in too much spirits. So you see that there is some justice in the world, after all!

KARLSTADT: But Luther has been excommunicated!

DOCTOR JOHANNES: What does that matter? Nobody would dare touch him! Maximilian, who abandoned him, died at just the right time. Don't you think you could say then that Luther has the protection of Providence? And now Luther's friend, the Elector, has been declared regent. So why do you complain?.

KARLSTADT: I wish I had never come to you. . . .

DOCTOR JOHANNES: Say something, contradict me, if you think I am wrong! But you can't—and that is why you rage. . . .

KARLSTADT: What will happen now?

DOCTOR JOHANNES: Do you take me for a wizard, a sorcerer, as the rabble seem to think? . . . I am merely a mathematician.

KARLSTADT: Perhaps you can figure out who will be the next emperor?

DOCTOR JOHANNES: Charles V, of course!—Because the Elector of Saxony has refused the throne—and because Charles has not only been proposed by the Elector, but he possesses the New World's gold to buy votes with! . . .

KARLSTADT: I don't believe it. . . .

DOCTOR JOHANNES: You are envious of Luther. . . .

KARLSTADT: I?

DOCTOR JOHANNES: Go in peace! Be a friend to your friend and don't touch his fate with heavy hand . . . for you do not understand what the future holds for him.

KARLSTADT: Luther has failed us!

DOCTOR JOHANNES: That's a lie! He fled in the face of overpowering odds in order to gather forces for new attacks! Go to Wittenberg—and you will see him in the vanguard—the greatest among them, and their leader, as he was here in Leipzig when you let yourself be beaten by Doctor Eck! . . . Go to Wittenberg—where we shall all meet. . . . Go!

KARLSTADT: I shall go—but I go my own way!

DOCTOR JOHANNES: Your own way—on others' errands!

KARLSTADT: Are you a papist?

DOCTOR JOHANNES: I don't know what that is. . . . I am a spectator who retains his common sense when the rest lose theirs. I am nothing that you think I may be—and you can give me no name that fits me. Everything you utter is empty sound—and the roads you take do not lead to where you imagine! He who is, has been and shall remain, smiles at you, but he uses you. Remember these words! It is not Luther, or Zwingli, or Calvin who will defeat the pope! It is the Emperor who shall do it! Emperor Charles V! And when that is done, Luther will be proclaimed pope in Rome!

KARLSTADT: Now I shall have to leave! . . .

(*Doctor Johannes continues with his writing.*)

End of Act Three

Act IV

In Wittenberg: outside the Elster Gate. On the left, the Elster Gate; on the right, an inn. Tables and chairs outside. Seated round a table are Ulrich von Hutten, Lucas Cranach, Amsdorff, Schurff, Melanchthon, and several men of learning. A miniature barrack theater has been erected in the rear.

ULRICH VON HUTTEN: Here we are gathered again!

LUCAS CRANACH: This time Brother Martin is offering us a new drama.

AMSDORFF: Up there, you mean?
(*He points to the theater.*)

LUCAS CRANACH: I don't know whether there is an epilogue. But Martin Luther never has any difficulty getting an audience . . . all he has to do is to beat the drum. . . .

ULRICH VON HUTTEN: But where is Martin's *alter ego* —Karlstadt?

MELANCHTHON: Andreas, they say, is out in the countryside, preaching.

LUCAS CRANACH: And what about Sachs? Hans Sachs?

ULRICH VON HUTTEN: He is at home, I presume, writing songs in praise of the new emperor. . . .

LUCAS CRANACH: The emperor, yes—nineteen years old! A new age is dawning!—Hail to the emperor— may he long live! To Charles V!

ALL: Hail! Long live Emperor Charles V!

ULRICH VON HUTTEN: Silence! The drama begins. . . .

THE PLAY:

(The Shoemaker enters.)

THE COOK *(Female)*: Honorable Canon! The shoe-maker is here.

THE CHOIRMASTER: A, *beneveneritis*, Master Hans!

THE SHOEMAKER: *Deo gratias.*

THE CHOIRMASTER: What! You come with my shoes?

THE SHOEMAKER: Yes, I thought you had already left for church.

THE CHOIRMASTER: No, I was back there in the green-house, doing some chores.

THE SHOEMAKER: Doing some chores?

THE CHOIRMASTER: Yes, I was rattling off my Horas and feeding my nightingale.

THE SHOEMAKER: What kind of nightingale have you, good sir? Can he still sing?

THE CHOIRMASTER: No, it's too late in the year.

THE SHOEMAKER: I know a shoemaker who has a nightingale that is only just beginning to warble.

THE CHOIRMASTER: The devil take that shoemaker and his nightingale. Think how he has squeezed and pinched the Holy Father, the holy dignitaries, and all of us venerable worthies!

THE SHOEMAKER: Oh no! He has only given you a pinch in your bellies and your money pouches!

THE CHOIRMASTER: I hear the bells in the sanctuary. . . . Cook, give me my coat! Go in peace, Master Shoemaker, and may all be well with you. . . .

THE SHOEMAKER: Amen!   *(He departs.)*

THE CHOIRMASTER: I believe the devil has flown into the shoemaker!—He won't be getting any more work from me—I'll give it to Hans Zobel instead . . . he has no Lutheranism or heresy in him!—Now, cook, I want you to go to the market square—get me a little bird—get me a dozen—the chaplain is coming to a little festivity—he and some of our friends. . . . Take the Bible out of the dining hall, and make sure there are dice and chips in the table drawer. . . . And don't forget a fresh deck of cards . . . better have two. . . .

The Curtain Falls

. . . . .

ULRICH VON HUTTEN: The voice is Jacob's—but the hands are Hans Sachs's! Hans!

ALL: Sachs! Come out, Sachs! Author!

(*Hans Sachs enters.*)

ALL: Hail! Hans Sachs!

HANS SACHS: Thank you, good friends!

LUCAS CRANACH: Let's have a duel between the two singers—Von Hutten and Sachs!

ULRICH VON HUTTEN: I am for it!—Hans is a worthy opponent—I accept the challenge! Who is to start?

LUCAS CRANACH: Sachs begins!

HANS SACHS: That's too great an honor—to sing where Ulrich von Hutten sings—and then, to compete with him, too! But the subject, good sirs!

LUCAS CRANACH: There is only one subject here in Wittenberg! It's Martin Luther, of course!

ALL: Good!—Martin Luther!

HANS SACHS   (*Recites*):

Wake up, you people, dawn is here
and night and shadows disappear. . . .
I hear a nightingale so rare
that sings within the clearing there;
the night is setting in the West,
the East with light is being blessed:
the red of dawn, the purple rays,

break barely through the misty haze . . .
the sun shines forth in bright array;
the moon's orbicular face grows wan —
the light it sent the flock is gone. . . .
The sheep, athirst, are led to water holes—but stray
and, frightened, scatter o'er the heath, then fled . . .
they'd lost their shepherd—he who watched o'er them—
    and led!
ALL: Excellent, Sachs! Now it's Von Hutten's turn!
ULRICH VON HUTTEN   (*Recites*):
How long will you bide in the valley below and
    benumb
men already drowsy, you deadening wind from the
    south?
From an alien land you came, fondling the hands and
    cheeks of the dumb,
lewdly to rob us of manhood and leave us in barren
drought. . . .
But threatening clouds draw near in north! From house
    to house, from every door,
is heard a cry! The mighty north wind starts a wave
that roars from inland to the farthest shore. . . .
It tears with terror, tears from town to peasant cave. . . .
It shakes the rotten apple, inert from foul decay;
the healthy fruit, however, lives: the law in nature has
    its source. . . . .
And when the bitter north wind has run its cleansing
    course,
then we can live and breathe again—and greet a new,
    a better day!

Because of the intricate rhymes and meter in this poetic passage, I have taken the liberty of translating it freely, without, however, sacrificing its inherent metaphorical sense or values.
    A.P.

THE DOMINICAN (*Comes up to Hans Sachs; he interrupts Von Hutten*): Does that contraption there belong to you?   (*He indicates the barrack theater.*)

HANS SACHS: Yes, it's mine.

THE DOMINICAN: Take it away! It's standing on church property!—Besides, shoemaker, stick to your last!

HANS SACHS (*Pointing to the puppet theater*): That is my last! Where is yours?

THE DOMINICAN: You are playing slippery stuff, my friend!

HANS SACHS: Leather like that needs a little grease.

ULRICH VON HUTTEN: Drive away the monk! He is Doctor Eck's secretary.

ALL: Doctor Eck's!

ULRICH VON HUTTEN: He who brought the ban from Rome!—Listen, monk! Didn't I once throw you out through a window? Didn't I? At Castle Ebernburg—at Von Sickingen's?

THE DOMINICAN: That's a lie!

ULRICH VON HUTTEN: If you say it's a lie, I'll take an oath that it's the truth!

(*Students enter, led by Leonhard Kaiser.—All carry wood logs and fagots which they pile in a heap.*)

THE DOMINICAN: What are you planning to do? This is the property of the Church—and I forbid any desecration of it. . . .

ULRICH VON HUTTEN: Students, sing a serenade to the monk—he is Doctor Eck's secretary!

THE STUDENTS (*With the exception of Kaiser, all form a ring round the Dominican, while shouting*):
Doctor Eck, Eck, Eck
is a fool and a quack!
He spouts ink with a peck. . . .
Let us put him in a sack!

Let us tar him, put him on the rack,
break his neck and feather his back!
Doctor Eck!

(Leonhard Kaiser lights the pyre.)
*(Students enter, carrying folios and tomes that they place
on the fire.)*

ULRICH VON HUTTEN: What are you doing?

LEONHARD KAISER: *Hoc est corpus—juris canonici!*
Here are the papal decretals, gratifications, Clementines,
Isidorians, and extravagants—and at least half of them are
counterfeits and forgeries. These are the chains with which
Rome has enslaved Germania since the days of Nero and
Claudius. . . .

ULRICH VON HUTTEN: Who are you?

LEONHARD KAISER: I myself am of no account . . . but
my name is Leonhard Kaiser and I have been called Martin
Luther's youngest friend—that is my most cherished distinc-
tion.

THE DOMINICAN: Sacrilege! Put out the fire!

LEONHARD KAISER: No! This is a fire that will never
be put out. . . . Can't you feel it?

THE STUDENTS *(Roar out)*:
Roast a goose and you get goose;
roast one whole, you'll nothing lose;
skin one and you get no gravy!

ALL: No gravy!

THE STUDENTS:
Roast a swan—and you get hell;
riot breaks as by a knell—
it gets hot. . . . Now is that right?

ALL: Is that right?

LEONHARD KAISER: Our leader is here!

ALL: Luther is coming! *(They all rise.)*
(The Dominican flees.)

(*Martin Luther enters. In one hand he holds the papal bull.
—In passing Leonhard Kaiser he pats him on the shoulder.*)

ALL: Hail, Luther!

MARTIN LUTHER   (*Motions for silence*): Because you
have grieved the holy of the Lord, you shall have grief and
be consumed by the eternal fire!

DOCTOR JOHANNES: Amen!

ALL: Amen!

LUCAS CRANACH: Come and sit down with your
friends now. . . .

MARTIN LUTHER: Not yet—it is too early to rest! . . .
But where is Karlstadt?

AMSDORFF: He is out on his own.

MARTIN LUTHER: Judas Iscariot!

LEONHARD KAISER   (*Kneels before Luther*): Take me
in his stead, Master. . . .

MARTIN LUTHER: Silence, blasphemer! I am a mere
apprentice myself—but I shall take you for the sake of your
earnest face, and you shall help me and be a stoker for our
Lord! . . . But why do you come to me, young man?

LEONHARD KAISER: Because—because . . . primarily
because you know how to forgive an enemy!

MARTIN LUTHER: I never forgive an enemy—not before I have broken arms and legs off him. . . .

LEONHARD KAISER: Learned and noble men—listen to
me! When Tezel, the indulgence salesman, was divested of
his office and threatened with imprisonment for thievery,
Doctor Luther wrote to him and gave him solace!

MARTIN LUTHER: You have to feel sorry for Satan,
too, don't you? And we are human, aren't we?—I must go
now! . . .

ULRICH VON HUTTEN: Where are you going?

MARTIN LUTHER: Quo vadis? I am going—to be crucified. . . .

LUCAS CRANACH: Where?

MARTIN LUTHER: I am told I am to appear before the emperor at the diet in Worms.

ULRICH VON HUTTEN: Don't go!

MARTIN LUTHER: Have you been in Worms? Have you been in the monastery there?

ULRICH VON HUTTEN: No, but I know the emperor! He has the pope hidden underneath his mantle.

MARTIN LUTHER: Then I have a chance to kill two birds with one stone!—Who wants to come with me?

AMSDORFF AND SCHURFF: We!

MARTIN LUTHER: Amsdorff! Schurff! Good names— both of them!

ULRICH VON HUTTEN: If you are going to Worms, I am not coming with you. But I shall be at your heels with my four hundred knights that I have gathered together....

MARTIN LUTHER: Sheathe your sword, Ulrich, and fight with your pen instead! Our weapons are the weapons of the spirit! Only of the spirit! You know what we are fighting against? Against all worldly, temporal, political power!

HANS SACHS: Let me clasp your hand, Martin!

MARTIN LUTHER: Indeed you may, Hans! And let youth have its fling—but don't expect me to go screaming and cavorting through the streets in this garb. No—later, later! Now I am going to the theologians—and you don't like theology. . . . Therefore—farewell: Lucas—Ulrich—Hans —Philip. . . . Farewell—all of you!   (*He leaves.*)

ALL (*Wave him farewell*): Farewell, Martin Luther!

MARTIN LUTHER: Look after the fire, Leonhard!—And you, Philip Melanchthon—you go home and write!

End of Act Four

Act V

Scene I

*The reception room outside the Council Chamber at Worms.
Soldiers and lackeys stand at the entrance to the chamber,
rear.*
*Martin Luther is seen at the window, left, his back to the
audience.*
*In the foreground, a stove ornamented with a figure of
Laocoön.*

FIRST SOLDIER: He doesn't look so dangerous, that
monk. . . .

SECOND SOLDIER: He'll be a good one to collect relics
from. . . .

FIRST SOLDIER: He looks like a bone picker who has
picked himself up on some trash heap!

(*The Lackeys laugh boisterously.*)

SECOND SOLDIER: And yet he drinks something terrible. . . . The moment he had finished burning the papal
bull, he sat down with some shoemakers and tailors and
started to booze.

FIRST SOLDIER: You saw him drink?

SECOND SOLDIER: No—but I heard about it—from
someone.

FIRST SOLDIER: Well—this time he'll get his back
broken, don't worry!

THE HERALD (*Enters; to the soldiers*): Is that the
king of the Jews?   (*The Lackeys laugh.*)

FIRST SOLDIER: He is the emperor of emperors!

THE HERALD   (*To Luther*): Turn around, monk!

(Martin Luther does not move.)

THE HERALD: Turn around, monk, and let me see if you can look people in the eye!

(Martin Luther turns and fixes his eyes on the Herald.)

THE HERALD   (*With a sign of fear*): Why—he looks—he looks like the devil!—However, when now the papal legate Aleander comes, you throw yourself down on your knees, you understand! . . .

MARTIN LUTHER: I'll do nothing of the kind!

THE HERALD: That alone ought to take care of him! —Well, then the soldiers will see to it that your face is on the floor!

MARTIN LUTHER: They'll do nothing of the sort! I came here under a safe conduct from the emperor. It is he who has summoned me—not the pope.

THE HERALD: Johann Huss came to Constance under a safe conduct, too—but both he and his safe conduct went up in smoke.—A safe conduct is given by grace and not for merit—isn't that right, eh? And a grace can be forfeited—isn't that right, eh?—Do you think I have read my Luther now, do you?   *(Martin Luther is silent.)*

THE HERALD: And I can tell you more. . . .

FIRST SOLDIER: The people want to take a look at the monk. . . . Is that permitted?

THE HERALD: Why, certainly! They can even spit in his face if they want to. . . . Let them come!

(The People in the doorway; they titter and giggle, pointing their fingers at Luther.)

THE HERALD: Step inside, good people, and take a good look at the bear. Yes—that's what he calls himself when he writes. This is how he writes, the saintly one: "You shall always find Luther like a bear on your road and like a lion on your path. From all sides he shall hurl himself upon you, and shall leave you no peace until he has crushed your iron skulls and transformed your copper foreheads into dust."—Sounds funny, doesn't it? (*The People laugh.*)

SECOND SOLDIER: The defendant's attorney, Doctor Hieronymus Schurff, asks permission to come in.

THE HERALD: Schurff? That's a dignified name for an attorney to a monk! Let in the keeper of the wild animal!
> (*Schurff enters. He goes up to Luther.*)
> (*The People withdraw and leave.*)

SCHURFF: Well, Martin, where are you now?

MARTIN LUTHER: In the snake pit!—But where are you, where is our cause—where is God in Heaven?

SCHURFF: I am not abandoning you, Martin—even though our cause is desperate!

MARTIN LUTHER: So—you are abandoning me now? Very well. . . .

SCHURFF: I said no. . . .

MARTIN LUTHER: Why is our case desperate?

SCHURFF: Because a friend of our cause—who is *your* enemy, Duke George of Saxony—has used up all your ammunition!

MARTIN LUTHER: What do you mean?

SCHURFF: When the diet convened, the duke submitted all the German nations' complaints against Rome, baring the whole miserable situation so vividly, so forcefully that he won the approbation not only of the princes but of the emperor himself.

MARTIN LUTHER: Oh, well . . . then I am no longer needed. . . .

SCHURFF: Now—wait a moment. . . . The duke then proposed that an ecclesiastical council be convened—and this proposal resulted in the setting up of a committee by the diet.

MARTIN LUTHER: And what did he say about me?

SCHURFF: Nothing—your name wasn't mentioned.

MARTIN LUTHER: Erased, blotted out! What am I doing here, then?

SCHURFF: You are here to defend your teachings—or to recant!

MARTIN LUTHER: You want me to recant, to retract? —Why, the emperor is coming to hear what I have to say. . . .

SCHURFF: Yes—he wishes to hear you recant!

MARTIN LUTHER: The devil he will!

SCHURFF: Martin!

MARTIN LUTHER: And if I don't recant? . . .

(Schurff does not answer.)

MARTIN LUTHER: . . . then he'll cancel my safe conduct?   *(Schurff remains silent.)*

MARTIN LUTHER: Then I am to be the sacrificial goat! . . . Very well!—Now my position is clear—and I like order and forthrightness in everything. . . . If I had any possessions I would make my will, and then send for someone to wash the body. . . .

SCHURFF: Martin—do not abandon our great cause. . . .

MARTIN LUTHER: If God turns away from our cause, then it is bound to go to hell—and I'll go into the fire—head first. . . . Why should I defend Him, if He will not defend me?

SCHURFF: Martin! This is your first trial—and you let yourself be defeated! Why—this is merely a trial, a test!

MARTIN LUTHER: How can I be sure it is? I would take it as a warning to retrace my steps! If God tells me: "Forward, Martin!"—then I go forward. . . . If He tells me to lie down, I lie down! I am not one to resort to circumlocution, to subterfuge, or pleasantries. . . .

SCHURFF: How you talk . . . how you talk! You really deserve to be burned as a blasphemer, not to say a heretic!

MARTIN LUTHER: Out of my sight, you apostle of Satan!

SCHURFF: Ssh! Ssh! . . . I am going direct to the table for the legal advocates—there is where you'll find me. . . . But remember one thing: from now on the fight before the diet is not between Luther and the Pope! The question is Germany or Rome! And the password for the day is: *Hic* Ghibellines, *Hic* Guelfs!—I know it is hard for you to swallow your arrogance, Luther, but it is time that it should be checked!

MARTIN LUTHER: Nonsense! What would Luther be without his arrogance?

SCHURFF (*Smiles*): Yes, I wonder? You are right!—Remain as you are! You are best that way!

(*With a nod, he leaves, right.*)

THE HERALD: The papal legate Aleander!

ALEANDER (*Enters, steps up to Luther and inspects him through his lorgnette*): This is the god Luther, isn't it?

MARTIN LUTHER: And you are the devil Aleander, aren't you?

ALEANDER (*Drops his lorgnette, which he picks up. Then to the Herald*): Have you a muzzle?

MARTIN LUTHER: No, but we have dog whips! And we have something still better. We have the Lord's sacred words, unspoiled by decretals and *corpus juris*. . . . We have common sense and a sense of justice. . . . We have God in our hearts and a clean conscience! What have you? Fire and smoke and empty nothingness—and the forgiveness for sins for ten ducats! I am blowing my breath on you now!

ALEANDER: Martin Luther! You are in error when you treat me like an enemy!

MARTIN LUTHER: Not even the devil would have you as a friend!

ALEANDER: You may not know it, but I disapproved of your being called here.

MARTIN LUTHER: Yes—you were afraid of me!

ALEANDER: Yes. . . . I was afraid that you would destroy our common aim—the aim of our Christendom: the re-creation of the Church.

MARTIN LUTHER: Indeed! Have we anything in common?

ALEANDER: Why not help us . . . in such a way, of course, that we can work together?

MARTIN LUTHER: You want me to help you?

ALEANDER: Aren't we endowed with the same spirit?

MARTIN LUTHER: I'll settle with your spirit by a smack on the snout!

ALEANDER: You bite when you are being patted, don't you?

MARTIN LUTHER: I don't like being patted by hippopotami and rattlesnakes! I am a Saxonian of iron miner stock and I am used to iron fists. Waste no slippery, oily words on me—I don't fall for false friends and touch neither them nor greased rods. . . . And if they try to pat me on the cheek, I bite. We are enemies! Now you know it!

ALEANDER: Yes, now I know it!—And you will find out what that means!
(*He goes toward the right, but turns and speaks to Luther.*)
Shall I send you my confessor?

MARTIN LUTHER: Why?

ALEANDER: In case you have a last wish. . . .
(*Martin Luther stands silent in despair.*)

ALEANDER: . . . and in case you should like to lighten your conscience before you meet your Judge?—The One who judges the living and the dead. . . .

MARTIN LUTHER (*In anguish*): Is that to be the judgment—death?   (*Aleander nods affirmatively and goes out.*)

MARTIN LUTHER: *Es cadaver!*

AMSDORFF   (*Enters excitedly and goes to Luther*):
Martin, your cause is lost—but there is one way to save
you! . . .

MARTIN LUTHER: And what is that?

AMSDORFF: Sickingen and Von Hutten have a band
of soldiers. . . .

MARTIN LUTHER: I fled once. . . . I shall never flee
again!

AMSDORFF: You will burn at the stake!

MARTIN LUTHER: If that's my fate—so be it!

AMSDORFF: Think of what you are doing!

MARTIN LUTHER: Go away, tempter! I am not eager
to die, but if I must, then I commend my spirit in Your
hands, Christ Jesus, Saviour of the world! Amen!

AMSDORFF: Amen!

(*The Herald strikes the floor with his lance. The Soldiers
come to attention.*)

AMSDORFF: The emperor is coming!

(*The doors, rear, are opened wide. The Emperor and the
Elector enter.*)

(*The Emperor disregards Luther. He stops and whispers
briefly to the Elector.*)

THE ELECTOR   (*Walks over to Luther*): Our most
gracious Lord and Emperor desires to know whether the
rumor abroad is true. . . . Have you recanted?

MARTIN LUTHER   (*With firmness*): No!

THE ELECTOR: Are you going to?

MARTIN LUTHER   (*In a thunderous voice*): No!

(*The Emperor enters the chamber, right, without having
paid any attention to Luther, and without waiting for the
Elector.*)

(*The Elector presses Luther's hand significantly and en-
couragingly; then whispers something in his ear and smiles.*

*—He walks to the door, right, surveys the chamber with
a glance, then turns, beckoning to Luther to enter the council chamber. An imperial fanfare is heard from within.)
(Martin Luther walks with a firm step toward the council
chamber and enters.)*

End of Scene One

Scene II

*The home of Luther's parents at Möhra.
Jacob Luther sits reading by the light of a miner's lantern.
It is night.*

MARTIN LUTHER   (*Enters. He is shabbily dressed, and
his clothes are wet. He is in his bare feet and bareheaded*):
Don't be frightened, Jacob . . . it is I—your brother Martin. . . .

JACOB: Oh, God in Heaven, is it you?

MARTIN LUTHER: I am homeless, hunted by the emperor's soldiers on horseback. Find me a place to rest. . . .
Are father and mother asleep?

JACOB: Yes, they are asleep—I think.

MARTIN LUTHER: Have you any water?

JACOB: No—and I wouldn't dare go after any . . . if
father should wake up he would kill you.—Where do you
come from?

MARTIN LUTHER: I just came from Worms and was on
my way to Wittenberg. . . . But I lost my way, and the
emperor's soldiers are at my heels. . . .

JACOB: Oh, Martin! And you have been excommunicated, too!

MARTIN LUTHER: Is that why you don't ask me to sit down?

JACOB: No! But father. . . .

MARTIN LUTHER: Oh? . . . Yes. . . .

JACOB: Be still! I can hear him! Yes! Go, Martin, go before he comes. . . .

MARTIN LUTHER: No! I am staying!

JACOB: He will kill you!

MARTIN LUTHER: I don't think he will. . . .

(*Father Luther enters from the right. He regards Martin Luther.*)

MARTIN LUTHER: Do you know me, father?

FATHER LUTHER: Yes, but I don't want to know you!

MARTIN LUTHER: I thank you!

FATHER LUTHER: That is how my own child answers me!

MARTIN LUTHER: I am not your child because I am not a child any longer! But I am your son—and that is why you have to give me a roof over my head tonight!

FATHER LUTHER: You haven't changed in the slightest!

MARTIN LUTHER: Nor have you!

FATHER LUTHER: The tongue of a snake! If I had a red-hot iron I would burn it out!

MARTIN LUTHER: Then will you as a Christian lend a room to a stranger?

FATHER LUTHER: If you were a stranger, yes . . . even if you were a Turk! But you are worse than a heathen, for you have broken with everything that binds us together. . . .

MARTIN LUTHER: I have broken all fetters. . . . You hear that, Jacob? You are free!

FATHER LUTHER: You have done away with all the old. . . .

MARTIN LUTHER: I have done away with all that was old, Jacob!—Be young, be alive and live!

FATHER LUTHER: . . . All that we revered. . . .

MARTIN LUTHER: . . . we now despise, because it was odious and decayed!

FATHER LUTHER: Jacob, do you think that this corrupted human being has any feelings?

MARTIN LUTHER: Jacob knows that I once had feelings, but you beat them out of me. And perhaps you did a good thing—for I have felt better without feelings. Today I am totally insensitive—no attacks can hurt me any more, thanks to the grace of God.

FATHER LUTHER: Your mother is in there. . . .

(*He points.*)

MARTIN LUTHER: And my father is in here—it is all the same to me! I was excommunicated because I did the righteous thing—and that is to my credit!

FATHER LUTHER: But your excommunication has been pronounced—you are outlawed—you are at the mercy of any and all—and that means infamy and disgrace!

MARTIN LUTHER: Have—the bans—been—pronounced?

FATHER LUTHER: You didn't know that, eh?

MARTIN LUTHER: I didn't know that!

FATHER LUTHER: And whoever houses you under his roof is equally guilty and will get the same punishment. . . .

MARTIN LUTHER: So—the bans have been published!

FATHER LUTHER: I hope you end on the gallows so that I won't have to see you burning at the stake.

JACOB: Father, father!

MARTIN LUTHER: Frank speech was always a virtue in this house, and the tradition is being carried on. . . . I am proud of you, my father; and you can be just as proud of your son, for he has not degenerated. . . .

JACOB: Martin! Martin!

MARTIN LUTHER: Now I am leaving . . . and I trust

that—some day—you will feel sorry for your conduct. I forgive you—for you know no better. . . .

FATHER LUTHER: You forgive me, you beggar—but I never forgive!

MARTIN LUTHER: Then you are a heathen, a pagan!
                                  (*Father Luther is silent.*)

MARTIN LUTHER: But you are a man, and I admire you!   (*Father Luther remains silent.*)

MARTIN LUTHER: I could almost swear that you don't despise me—the one and only man who has dared look you in the white of the eye. . . . I am going now—out in the night—into the rain—into the darkness of the woods—into the hands of the imperial soldiers. . . .

FATHER LUTHER: Yes, go to hell from where you came!

MARTIN LUTHER: So be it! I would like to shake your hand. . . .

FATHER LUTHER: Have you no shame!

MARTIN LUTHER: Like father, like son!

FATHER LUTHER   (*With a smile*):   By my soul, if I don't believe you *are* my son!—Give me your fist!

MARTIN LUTHER   (*Extends his hand*):   Steel against steel—the steel of Saxony.

FATHER LUTHER: Sit down now, and behave like a human being. . . .

MARTIN LUTHER: No, thank you, father—I have friends who are waiting for me at the inn. I only wanted to step inside and give you a handclasp.—Give my love to mother—and a kiss from me right smack on her mouth!—And may God be with you and your home—and with me!
                                          (*He leaves.*)

End of Scene Two

Scene III

Wartburg Castle.—Luther's study.
In the rear, a door opening onto his bedroom, where he is
seen walking about, disturbed and unable to sleep. He is
dressed as a young nobleman and goes by the name of
George.
It is night.
Berlepsch is reclining in a chair, half asleep.
The castle clock strikes three times.

THE STEWARD   (*Enters; to Berlepsch*): Are you asleep,
captain?

BERLEPSCH: No, how can I sleep?

THE STEWARD: He is a difficult guest, that doctor. . . .

BERLEPSCH: Just so you won't forget, call him "squire."

THE STEWARD: Has he had any sleep tonight?

BERLEPSCH: No, he keeps praying, and talks aloud to
himself . . . and, believe me or not—I heard him battling
with someone in there. . . .

THE STEWARD: Yes—he is sick—and he is having visions. . . . How long do you suppose we shall have to put
up with him?

BERLEPSCH: I have no idea—nor have you—nor he—
nor anyone else. He himself doesn't know whether he is a
prisoner or not.

THE STEWARD: Thanks to our wise Elector—that's the
way he wants it. The bear had to be tamed, and caged for
a while, until he cooled down. I dare say these nine months
have done him much good.

BERLEPSCH: Is it really nine months? Well, that's just
the time it takes to be born, and he certainly needed to be
reborn!

THE STEWARD: But it must disturb him, don't you think, not to be kept informed of what is going on in the world outside—since we don't give him any dispatches?

BERLEPSCH: That was done for his own good—to give him rest and peace so that he could complete his work on the Bible. I must say the Elector knows what he is doing! He certainly does!

THE STEWARD: But can you imagine what he will say when he hears of the changes that have taken place in the world since the diet at Worms!

BERLEPSCH: I wouldn't like to be near him when he does! That man has a strength so powerful, so devastating, that I sometimes wonder whether the vaults and arches will be able to withstand his stentorian tones.

THE STEWARD: Think what will happen when he is set loose again . . . when he is set loose! . . .

BERLEPSCH: Have you heard about a wild scheme by the papists to sick a Delilah on our Samson?

THE STEWARD: On him! Don't worry, he could take care of half a dozen Delilahs! Besides, he wouldn't look at a woman!

BERLEPSCH: Well—but didn't he let out some of the nuns from the convent and quarter them in Wittenberg? Didn't he?

THE STEWARD: That man has time for everything. . . . He could defend this fortress with his pen better than our swords and mortars!

BERLEPSCH: If that man only knew what power he possesses . . . if he knew what he has accomplished already!

THE STEWARD: He seems to realize it at times—and then he takes on the stature of a Moses, when Moses asked to see God. . . .   (*The sound of a horn is heard.*)

BERLEPSCH: Visitors—in the middle of the night!

THE STEWARD: They are letting down the draw-

bridge! Then it must be an emissary from the Elector!—
Perhaps I had best go down and receive him. . . .
(He gets up.)

BERLEPSCH: Would you like a lantern for the stairs?

THE STEWARD: Thank you—but it's almost daylight. . . .   (He goes out.)

(Martin Luther enters the study. He looks around.)

BERLEPSCH: You don't get much sleep, squire, do you?

MARTIN LUTHER: No—I am reading Job. . . . "Am I
a sea, or a whale, that thou settest a watch over me? When
I say: My God shall comfort me, my couch shall ease my
complaint; then thou scarest me with dreams, and terrifiest
me through visions: so that my soul chooseth strangling,
and death rather than my life."— (There is a pause.)
—Will it soon be morning?

BERLEPSCH: Soon, doctor, soon!

MARTIN LUTHER: It makes me feel bad that you have
to sit up?

BERLEPSCH: It doesn't hurt—doesn't hurt. . . .

THE STEWARD (Enters): We have a guest.

BERLEPSCH: Who is it?

THE STEWARD: It's a Benedictine monk with a missive
from the Elector.

BERLEPSCH: For whom?

THE STEWARD: Squire George . . . together with a
verbal message from the Elector—to be delivered to him
personally.

BERLEPSCH: Can we be sure of the messenger?

THE STEWARD: He has identified himself by his cre-
dentials.

BERLEPSCH: Very well, let him come in!

(The Steward admits the Benedictine monk, dressed according to his order.)

BERLEPSCH: Welcome, Brother! Here is the squire!

(*To the monk.*) But choose your words carefully—the doctor is a sick man. . . . Good morning, Brother. . . .

(*Berlepsch and the Steward leave.*)

THE BENEDICTINE MONK: Can anyone overhear us?

MARTIN LUTHER: No—they are all honest here.

THE BENEDICTINE MONK: First of all—I want you to recognize me. . . .

MARTIN LUTHER: Doctor Johannes! What brings you here?

DOCTOR JOHANNES: I am carrying a missive of no importance from the Elector—merely as an excuse to have a talk with you!

MARTIN LUTHER: Give me the missive!

DOCTOR JOHANNES: There is nothing in it—and the time is short. . . .

MARTIN LUTHER   (*Glances through the missive*): Sit down!

(*Doctor Johannes takes a seat. Martin Luther sits down also.*)

Will you commence, or shall I?

DOCTOR JOHANNES: I'll let you begin. . . .

MARTIN LUTHER: Tell me frankly: Am I a prisoner here, or am I not?

DOCTOR JOHANNES: You are the Elector's guest and have never been anything else.

MARTIN LUTHER: Well—that makes the sky seem brighter. . . .

DOCTOR JOHANNES: Much has happened since that day in the library when I placed the Bible in your hand—and since I showed you Huss's writings in the monastery.

MARTIN LUTHER: You have had a finger in my fate—I can't deny that.—Who are you?

DOCTOR JOHANNES: You know who I am. . . . I am Doctor Faust who has lived more lives and read and

studied more than others—and therefore has been consid-
ered a magician, a sorcerer. . . .

MARTIN LUTHER: You read the future?

DOCTOR JOHANNES: Who doesn't? Doctor Reuchlin,
for example, is a great devotee of cabalism.

MARTIN LUTHER: That's an abomination, a satanic
abomination, and I don't want to know anything about it!

DOCTOR JOHANNES: Are you aware of your position in
Germany today?

MARTIN LUTHER: I am a dead man!

DOCTOR JOHANNES: You were for a time—while Leo X
was still alive.

MARTIN LUTHER: Is Leo dead?

DOCTOR JOHANNES: You didn't know?

MARTIN LUTHER: No!

DOCTOR JOHANNES: You didn't know. . . ?—They must
have kept it from you. . . .

MARTIN LUTHER: It looks that way! Who is pope
now?

DOCTOR JOHANNES: Adrian VI.

MARTIN LUTHER: What is he—fish or fowl?

DOCTOR JOHANNES: He was tutor to the Emperor—is
a friend of Erasmus—and he is now aiming to reform the
Roman Church.

MARTIN LUTHER: The devil, you say! Is the pope going to reform?

DOCTOR JOHANNES: Yes!—You ought to be proud of a
pope who is doing your work.

MARTIN LUTHER: I like to do my own work myself!

DOCTOR JOHANNES: Doctor Luther—you are as good
as pope in Rome.

MARTIN LUTHER: I'd rather be a professor in Wittenberg.—So—my work is going to be frittered away? . . . Perhaps already has been!

DOCTOR JOHANNES: Nothing of the sort! Your work is done—and the princes have now taken a hand in it themselves. . . . They are helping you!

MARTIN LUTHER: You come with news I know nothing about!—Where is the Emperor? Did he erect pyres and flames as he vowed he would?

DOCTOR JOHANNES: The Emperor left Germany after Worms.

MARTIN LUTHER: After Worms?

DOCTOR JOHANNES: Yes—there was rebellion in Spain —he was at war with the Turks—and now Francis I is on his neck, so that the princes in Germany can do as they please. Luther's books are being sold and read without hindrance; and no one pays any attention to bulls and bans any more.

MARTIN LUTHER: God is all-powerful! He rules, and we are mere harlequins and marionettes!—Tell me some more! More! This is like the tale of the deep-sleeper!

DOCTOR JOHANNES: Well—the monasteries are no longer sealed—the monks have been put to work—and the priests are marrying. . . .

MARTIN LUTHER: God is omnipotent! God is beneficent and gracious—and I am a worm!—More!

DOCTOR JOHANNES: Karlstadt is married—Feldkirchen has taken himself a wife. . . .

MARTIN LUTHER: Karlstadt? That Judas! What is he doing?

DOCTOR JOHANNES: We are coming to him in a moment. . . . . By and large, it might be said, then, that the cause has been victorious and that the whole of Germany is set free.

MARTIN LUTHER: O God, I thank you! What an ungrateful wretch I have been! But why wasn't I told? Here

I have been walking about, grumbling, as the children of Israel did!

DOCTOR JOHANNES: But now we come to the stumbling blocks. You have to be prepared for a few of those, too. . . .

MARTIN LUTHER: Go on!

DOCTOR JOHANNES: That your teachings should be distorted and the word *freedom* be given many meanings, and be misunderstood—for *that* I was prepared. But you were not!

MARTIN LUTHER: Speak out!

DOCTOR JOHANNES: Well—in Wittenberg there have appeared prophets who—interpreting the Bible and your writings literally—are carrying on like savages. . . . They are disrupting divine services, plundering the churches, and living like pagans.

MARTIN LUTHER: That is the Iscariot Karlstadt, isn't it?

DOCTOR JOHANNES: He is their leader, yes! And this movement is of danger to the great cause—and the Elector is now summoning you to preach against these disturbers, these lost sheep! It means, in a sense, that you will be preaching against yourself. . . .

MARTIN LUTHER: Against myself?

DOCTOR JOHANNES: Yes—to some extent. . . .

MARTIN LUTHER   (*Griefstricken*): I never meant any such thing. . . .

DOCTOR JOHANNES: No—but they misunderstood. . . . Show them the light! It will give you a chance to broaden your teachings a little, too.

MARTIN LUTHER: I shall pounce on them and punish them. I shall strike like lightning in broad daylight and steal on them like a thief in the night. I shall unmouth them with the biggest and loudest mouth in Germany. I shall

spike together their lying throats and beat their heads together until they fall apart! . . . If they will only let me out
of here!

DOCTOR JOHANNES: The gates are open! The sun is
rising!

MARTIN LUTHER   (*Exultant*): I can get out—I am
free! . . . "O Lord, I will praise Thee: though Thou wast
angry with me, Thine anger is turned away, and Thou com-
fortedst me!"—Are you coming with me?

DOCTOR JOHANNES: No, doctor. . . . We are at the
parting of the ways now. . . . The child has been born—
now raise it up! It is a long and arduous task. I was merely
the midwife!

MARTIN LUTHER: Godspeed to you! And I thank you
for the help you gave me!

DOCTOR JOHANNES: Thanks! . . . And live now with
the times! . . . I shall continue on—toward the unknown
future—that no doubt will resemble the present, yet not be
the same. . . .

MARTIN LUTHER   (*Facing the window*): See! The
day is dawning . . . over Thuringia!

DOCTOR JOHANNES: Over Germany!

End of Act Five

THROUGH DESERTS
TO ANCESTRAL LANDS
(MOSES)

Persons in the Play:

THE PRIEST
PHARAOH
JOCHEBED, the mother of Moses
MIRIAM, the sister of Moses
PHARAOH'S DAUGHTER
THE INFANT MOSES
MOSES
JETHRO, the father-in-law of Moses
THE VOICE
AARON, the brother of Moses
THE ISRAELITE
THE EGYPTIAN
JOSHUA
HUR
CALEB
SEVEN SCOUTS
KORAH
DATHAN
ABIRAM
BALAAM THE SOOTHSAYER
THE TWELVE ELDERS
People of Israel
Scouts

The Settings:

Scene I (The Prologue): *The Temple of The Sun God in Egypt*

Scene II: *Pharaoh's Garden*

Scene III: *A craggy region of Mount Sinai*

Scene IV: *The Temple of the Sun God*

Scene V: *By the Red Sea*

Scene VI: *In the desert*

Scene VII: *In the desert*

Scene VIII: *In the desert*

Scene IX: *Mount Sinai*

Scene X: *Mount Sinai, enclosed by a fence*

Scene XI: *On the crest of Mount Sinai*

Scene XII: *On the crest of Mount Sinai*

Scene XIII: *Mount Sinai (as in Scene IX)*

Scene XIV: *The Sanctuary of the Tabernacle*

Scene XV: *The fore-court of the Tabernacle*

Scene XVI: *In the desert*

Scene XVII: *In the desert*

Scene XVIII: *On top of a mountain in the desert*

Scene XIX: *In the desert*

Scene XX: *In the desert*

Scene XXI: *On Mount Nebo*

Scene I

THE PROLOGUE

The Temple of the Sun God in Egypt, with the Nile tide gauge. It is morning.

THE PRIEST: God of Sun, ruler of the shining sun! Be praised in the morning when you rise and in the evening when you set! . . . I invoke and worship you, Lord of Eternity, Sun of the Two Horizons—You, Creator, who have created yourself! All the gods fill the air with rejoicing when they behold you, King of the heavens. . . . I become young again when I see your beauty. . . . Hail, hail to you when you come to the Land of the living, you Father of the gods!

PHARAOH   (*Enters*): Already offering your prayers, you wisest among men of wisdom?

THE PRIEST: My sovereign has summoned me—and your servant has obeyed! My sovereign has returned to his land after many long and glorious campaigns of victory in strange and faraway countries.—Your servant bids you welcome with his countenance in the dust. . . .

PHARAOH: My chariots have rolled across the red soil of Syria—my horses have trampled the roads of Babylon and Nineveh: I crossed the Phrat and the Tigris and the land between the two rivers—I came to Sindh and to the Ganges where the boundaries of the land of silk begin, only to extend toward the rising sun; I turned about in my tracks and set out toward the north, to Scythia and Colchis. Wherever I came, I heard the murmur of voices and saw people

in movement. . . . The peoples had become awake; in the
temples there were prophecies of the return of the gods—
for men had been left to do their labors and to govern
themselves, their own fate—and they had performed their
tasks badly. . . . Right had become wrong, and truths had
turned into lies. . . . The entire world sighed for deliverance . . . finally their prayers reached the throne—the throne
of the All-Merciful One; and now the wise and the gentle,
the holy ones, are proclaiming in all tongues the joyous
message: The gods are returning! Returning to help the
children of humanity back to orderliness and sanity where
they have wrought chaos and confusion—to establish law
and order and vindicate justice.

This is the message I bring home with me as the booty of
victory, and you, the wisest among the wise, shall be the
first one to receive it from your sovereign. . . .

THE PRIEST: All that is spoken throughout the length
and breadth of the universe, you hear—your eye sees farther
than the stars of the heavens—sees farther than the eye of
the sun!

PHARAOH: And despite that—what the gods have
granted me to hear in dreams, my ear may have perceived
. . . but my mind has not comprehended. . . . I ask you to
interpret it for me. . . .

THE PRIEST: Tell it me, my sovereign!

PHARAOH: I saw nothing—but I heard a voice when
sleep had shut the light of my eye . . . and it spoke in the
dark and said: "The red soil shall be scattered throughout
the lands of the earth, but the black soil shall ebb away as
the sand in the seas."

THE PRIEST: Your dream, my sovereign, is not hard
to interpret. . . . But it bodes no good.

PHARAOH: Interpret it!

THE PRIEST: The red earth is Syria—you know that,

Sire! Syria or the land of Canaan is the ancestral land of the
Hebrews. . . . The black earth is the land of the Nile, your
land: Egypt. . . .

PHARAOH: Forever the Hebrews! Forever and always
the Hebrews!—Centuries have passed since this people
came into our land. They have multiplied, but they have
never given us cause for worry. I do not love them—neither
do I hate them . . . but now I am beginning to fear them.
They have labored hard—harder than ever of late—but they
have never complained or grumbled; they are a patient
people—as if they were waiting for something that were in
store for them—something that were to be. . . .

THE PRIEST: Give them their freedom, Sire!

PHARAOH: No—then they would set to work and
found a kingdom of their own.

THE PRIEST: Set them free!

PHARAOH: No—I want to be able to keep my eye on
them!

THE PRIEST: Give them freedom!

THE PHARAOH: No—I want to destroy them!

THE PRIEST: Set them free!

PHARAOH: No, I want to destroy them—that is a lesser
cruelty!—Yes—I want to destroy them!

THE PRIEST: But what about your dream, Sire?

PHARAOH: I interpret it as a warning and an exhortation.

THE PRIEST: Not, then, as a prophecy or a foreboding
of the inevitable—what is to come?

PHARAOH: No—as a warning and an exhortation. . . .

THE PRIEST: Do not touch that people, Sire, for their
God is stronger than ours!

PHARAOH: Their god is the god of the Chaldeans!
Very well! May our gods go to battle! I have spoken! You

have heard my words! I have nothing to add, and I take back nothing!

THE PRIEST: Sire, you see a sun on the firmament, and you know that it shines upon all peoples—the same sun! Don't you believe, too, that the Lord of the heavens is one and the same and that he rules over the fates of all mankind?

PHARAOH: That is the way it ought to be! But the Lord of the heavens has made me to rule over this land—and that is what I am now doing!

THE PRIEST: You are the ruler, Sire, but you have no power over wind and weather. It is not in your power to raise the water of the Nile by an inch, and there is nothing you can do to prevent our having another drought this year.

PHARAOH: Drought—famine? What does the tide gauge indicate?

THE PRIEST: Sire, the sun has entered the sign of the Scales, when the water normally begins to ebb. . . . The water level is down to three rods—and that forebodes famine. . . .

PHARAOH: If so it be, I shall do away with all unnecessary mouths to feed. I shall destroy the Hebrews!

THE PRIEST: Give them their liberty, Sire, and let them go in peace!

PHARAOH: I shall summon all midwives and command them to put to death all male children that are being born of Hebrew women. I have spoken—now I go to carry it out!

(*He leaves.*)

End of Scene I

Scene II

Pharaoh's Garden

A sluice gate, leading to the Nile, is visible.

(*Jochebed, the mother of Moses, is seen at the sluice gate.*)
(*Miriam, Moses' sister, appears in the center of the garden.*)

MIRIAM: Mother!

JOCHEBED: My daughter!

MIRIAM: We must hasten! Pharaoh's daughter is coming. . . . She is coming to bathe in the river.

JOCHEBED: Lord God of Israel, have mercy on my child!

MIRIAM: Have you suckled him?

JOCHEBED: Yes, I have!—The basket is floating among the bulrushes, but the river is flowing swiftly—it is red with blood and thick like curd. Oh Lord, God of Israel, have mercy upon my child!

MIRIAM: He will—just as he had mercy upon our Father Abraham and his seed when they went into the land of the Egyptians. Because he obeyed, Abraham was given the promise: "Through your seed all the peoples of the earth shall be blessed!" said the Lord.

JOCHEBED: And now Pharaoh is to slay all the first-born. . . .

MIRIAM: But not your son!

JOCHEBED: He has not yet!

MIRIAM: Pray, and hope!

JOCHEBED: Hope for what?—That the beasts of the river shall not devour him—that its surging water shall not swallow him up—that Pharaoh's headsmen shall not slay him. . . . That is my hope!

MIRIAM: The promise is greater, and it still lives! "Your seed shall occupy the enemies' gates."

JOCHEBED: Pharaoh's daughter is here!

MIRIAM: Have no fear! She is a friend of the defenseless, suffering Hebrews. . . .

JOCHEBED: She is her father's daughter. . . .

MIRIAM: The Egyptians are the children of our sisters and brothers. . . . They are the descendants of Ham; we are the descendants of Shem. Shem and Ham were brothers. . . .

JOCHEBED: But Ham was cursed by his father Noah . . . and Canaan was his son.

MIRIAM: But Noah said: "Praise be to the Lord, the God of Shem, and may Canaan be a servant of servants to his brethren!" Did you hear what I said? Shem was given the promise—and we are of Shem's seed!

JOCHEBED: Pharaoh's daughter is close upon us!

MIRIAM: The Lord God of Israel is *over* us! . . .

....

PHARAOH'S DAUGHTER   (*Enters with a slave girl*): Jochebed!

(*Jochebed falls on her knees and touches the ground with her face.*)

PHARAOH'S DAUGHTER: Jochebed! You have slaved for me in my garden, and the flowers have rejoiced and bloomed under your touch. . . . That proves to me that you are a good woman, Jochebed. I took a stroll on the roof of my father's palace to cool off—and from there I saw. . . .

(*Jochebed shows she is frightened.*)

PHARAOH'S DAUGHTER: I watched what you were doing. . . . I saw the basket among the bulrushes, Jochebed! Give me your offspring and let me care for him; then you will see whether *I* am a good woman also—if he thrives under my hand.   (*Jochebed rises.*)

PHARAOH'S DAUGHTER: Miriam! Fetch me the basket! (*Miriam goes over to the sluice gate, opens it and goes outside.—She returns with the basket.*)

PHARAOH'S DAUGHTER: Open the lid!
(*Miriam opens it.*)

PHARAOH'S DAUGHTER: What a beautiful child!—I have found it, and it is mine!   (*Jochebed strokes the child.*)

PHARAOH'S DAUGHTER: Now I must find a wet nurse! —Jochebed, you shall suckle my child. . . . Will you?
(*Jochebed kisses the hem of her garment.*)

PHARAOH'S DAUGHTER: Go in peace—I shall take care of your son!   (*Jochebed leans over the basket.*)

PHARAOH'S DAUGHTER: And may my son bring me happiness!

....

MIRIAM: The daughter of Pharaoh is to rear Jochebed's son! The children of Ham shall be the servants of Shem! Blessed be the Lord, the God of Shem!—You see the promise, mother, don't you? . . . The promise!

End of Scene II

Scene III

A craggy region of Mount Sinai (Horeb), covered by thickets

(Moses stands on a rock, carrying a staff; he is engrossed in prayer.)
(Jethro, the Midianite priest, father-in-law of Moses, is seen mounting another rock.)

JETHRO: Moses, my son, I have been seeking you!— What are you doing here on the Lord's mountain?

MOSES: Jethro, my father, is this Horeb, the Lord's Mountain?

JETHRO: Yes—and it is also called Sinai. . . . Where have you my sheep?

MOSES: How long am I to watch herd over your sheep?

JETHRO: As long as your gratitude lasts! You came as a refugee from Pharaoh's land. . . . I gave you protection— gave you my daughter Zipporah to wife . . . and still you complain!

MOSES: I am not complaining because of that. . . . But I am grieving for my brethren in the land of the Egyptians. . . . They are in dire need—and suffering hardships and afflictions. . . .

JETHRO: Are not the Midianites also among the children of Abraham? Are not your sons the sons of my daughter?

MOSES: So they are. But they who are well off must think of those who are suffering need. Israel is suffering and is being consumed in captivity by the Egyptians . . . and in the silent night beneath the stars I hear their wailing carried plaintively by the wind; and the sand in the desert whispers of their anguish and their pain. . . .

Dear father Jethro, let me depart for the west that I may see my father and mother, my brothers and sisters!

JETHRO: My son, go seek my sheep—seek your wife and your children—here! The sun is setting. . . . I am going to the temple to say my evening prayer. . . . We shall meet at the huts. The Lord of Sabaoth protect you and preserve you!   (*He leaves.*)

(*Moses kneels in prayer.*)

(*A bush is suddenly seen burning without being consumed by the flames.*)

THE VOICE: Moses! Moses!

MOSES: Here I am! . . .

THE VOICE: Do not tread here. . . . Remove your sandals—the ground whereupon you stand is consecrated ground!   (*Moses removes his sandals.*)

THE VOICE: I am the God of your fathers, the God of Abraham, the God of Isaac, and the God of Jacob!

(*Moses covers his face.*)

THE VOICE: I have witnessed the wailings of my people in Egypt—I have heard their lamentations and am descended to deliver them from the clutches of the Egyptians and lead them out of that land of Egypt into a good land and a vast land flowing with milk and honey. And that land is where the Canaanites, the Hittites, the Amorites, the Perizzites, the Hivites and the Jebusites live. Now that the cries of the children of Israel have reached me, you may go. I shall send you to Pharaoh and you shall lead my people, the children of Israel, out of Egypt.

MOSES: Who am I, Lord, that I should go to Pharaoh and lead the children of Israel out of Egypt?

THE VOICE: I shall be with you, and for you this shall

be a token that I have sent you: When you have led my people out of Egypt, you shall sacrifice to your God upon this mountain.

MOSES: But—when I come to the children of Israel and say to them: "The God of your fathers has sent me to you" . . . and they answer me: "What is His name?"—what shall I answer them?

THE VOICE: "I am that I am!"—And then you shall say to the children of Israel: "I AM has sent me unto you!"

MOSES: O Lord, I am a man slow of speech and of a slow tongue. . . .

THE VOICE: Be on your way. . . . I shall speak with your mouth and teach you what to say.

MOSES: Lord, send whomever you will, only not me.

THE VOICE (*In anger*): Do I not know that your brother Aaron of the tribe of Levi has a fluent tongue? He shall speak to the people for you.—Now go in peace!

End of Scene III

Scene IV

The Temple of the Sun, with the Nile tide gauge

The stage is dark.

THE PRIEST: Pharaoh, my sovereign, stand still—do not move—you are at the brink of the river, by the tide gauge! . . .

PHARAOH: Three days and three nights this darkness has prevailed. . . . Pray to the Ruler of the Sun that He again give us of his light!

THE PRIEST: Sire, I have prayed, but the God of the Hebrews is thwarting us!—Stand still where you are—or you will step on the snake!

PHARAOH: Where?

THE PRIEST: There—and there—and everywhere!—Do not move!

PHARAOH: Am I not in the Temple of the Sun? . . .

THE PRIEST: You are— yes. . . . Here is the river basin —the water in it is full of stinking blood—the fish is dead, and the locusts are rotting by the thousands.—Set Israel free!

PHARAOH: My father feared them, for he had been told in a dream that they would found a state of their own and destroy us.

THE PRIEST: Many years have passed since I stood here in the temple with your father, Sire! And I said to him then as I say to you now: Set Israel free!—But he did not listen to me. . . .

PHARAOH: Give me your hand—I am afraid. . . . What is the noise I hear? It rattles, it clatters, it rustles—I feel something soft under my foot—I am touching something hairy! . . . Help—Heavenly Ruler, help!

THE PRIEST: Stand still! It is the beasts of the earth that are crawling upon us—it is the monsters of the river. . . . Let Israel go free!

PHARAOH: No!

THE PRIEST: Then we shall all perish—but Israel will survive and have the power! Set Israel free!

PHARAOH: No!

THE PRIEST: Think of your first-born son!

PHARAOH: I do!

THE PRIEST: The God of the Hebrews will send His destroying angel!

PHARAOH: The destroying angel?

THE PRIEST: He who shall slay all our first-born—as your sovereign father once slew all of Israel's first-born!

PHARAOH: That is a lie! The Hebrews are lying!

THE PRIEST: Do you not see how pain and suffering are overtaking us—visited upon your people—while the Hebrews are spared? Their God is mightier than all our gods!

PHARAOH: Then pray to their God—offer up sacrifices to Him!

THE PRIEST: Do you really mean that, Pharaoh? If we abandon our gods, *they* will abandon *us* also; and the God of the Hebrews is not friendly to us.

PHARAOH: Summon Moses and Aaron—for the last time!

THE PRIEST: They are outside in the fore-court waiting for a sign!

PHARAOH: Give the sign!—No, wait! . . . What is this chill air sweeping about my feet?

THE PRIEST: Woe to us, the river is rising from the melting hail!

PHARAOH: Give the sign! . . . No—wait!—I see a glare that is penetrating the darkness. . . .

THE PRIEST: It is the prophet of the Hebrews, the godly Moses! He has spoken with God . . . that is why he radiates this light. . . .

PHARAOH: Give the sign!
(The Priest blows a trumpet.)

....

(A faint glimmer spreads over the stage. The water recedes and the beasts flee.)

MOSES   (*Enters. His face radiates light; but otherwise darkness pervades*): Speak, Aaron!

AARON   (*Who has come in with Moses*): You have summoned us, Sire!

PHARAOH: What is it you request?

MOSES: Speak, Aaron. . . .

AARON: Set Israel free!

PHARAOH: Then *our* freedom would be at an end!

MOSES: Speak, Aaron!

AARON: The land of Egypt is already on the wane, and Canaan is now in the ascendant. . . .

PHARAOH: Very well! Depart from my nation, you and your children of Israel! Go, all of you, but leave your blessing upon me, you child of humanity, who has spoken with God!

MOSES: May God bless you and keep you!
(He stretches out his hands and it grows light.)

PHARAOH: The sun is shining again—there is light over the earth—and the spirit rejoices!—Stay here one day longer that we may all rejoice together!

MOSES: Speak, Aaron!

AARON: Let Israel go—at once!—Let there be no delay!

PHARAOH: No!

AARON: If you let your heart harden again, cowardly Pharaoh, the destroying angel shall stalk your land. . . .

(*Moses stretches out his hands; it grows dark again, and the Destroying Angel appears with Pharaoh's first-born son.*)

PHARAOH: (*Falls to his knees and touches the ground with his face*): Depart, Israel!

THE PRIEST: Now it has come to pass—and the promise that was given in the beginning of time shall be fulfilled: Ham shall be the servant of Shem, and the sons of Japheth shall share in the promise.

MOSES (*Stretches out his hand; again there is light*): Aaron, my brother, and all of Israel! When your children some day in years to come ask you about this, you shall answer: "The Lord led us with His almighty hand out of the house of bondage in Egypt."

End of Scene IV

Scene V

By the Red Sea

A pillar of a cloud is visible on high.

(*Moses is seen standing on a rock on the shore.*)

THE ISRAELITE   (*Enters*): Pharaoh is upon us with his army! He is aiming to drive us into the Red Sea!

MOSES: Let him come!

THE ISRAELITE: Were there no graves in Egypt? Why did you bring us to the desert to die?

MOSES: Have no fear! Stand firm and you will see what bliss the Lord will heap upon you this very day . . . for when this day is ended you shall never lay eyes upon the Egyptians again unto eternity! The Lord is waging the battle for you, and you shall not have to move a finger.

THE ISRAELITE: Behold, the cloud is sinking!

MOSES: Fall upon your face, my child! The Lord is about to speak!   (*The Israelite does as Moses commands.*) (*Moses covers his face. The pillar of a cloud descends upon the water.*)

THE VOICE: Why are you calling to me?—Lift up your staff, stretch out your hand over the sea and separate the water that the children of Israel may walk across on dry land! . . . And I will harden the hearts of the Egyptians so that they will follow you and pursue you!

(*The pillar of a cloud turns dark, its edges flaming with fire. The whole of the stage is in darkness, but Moses' countenance shines with light. He stretches forth his staff, and an ominous rumbling is heard.*)

....

THE EGYPTIAN   (*Enters*): Let us flee from Israel! The Lord is fighting for them against the Egyptians!

(*He hastens out.*)

....

THE VOICE: Stretch out your hand over the sea that the water may swallow up the Egyptians!

(*Moses stretches out his hand.*)

(*The pillar of a cloud is transformed into a pillar of fire resembling a colossus of an old man.*)

MOSES: I will sing the praises of the Lord for He has done a glorious deed. The Lord is my strength and my song of praise! He is my bliss; He is my God. . . . I will honor and bless Him. . . . He is the God of my father, and I will exalt Him. His name is the Lord! The enemy said: "I will pursue them and seize them and plunder and take booty and satisfy my courage upon them." . . . And they all sank in the water like lead. . . .

Let fear and fright grip them, and awe of Your powerful arm, until Your people have come safely across, O Lord,— until Your people have escaped all that from which You have delivered them! . . .

Lead them and plant them upon the mountain of Your heritage, which You, O Lord, have chosen as Your dwelling place!—May the Lord reign in eternity, days without end!

THE VOICE: If you will hearken to the Voice of the Lord, your God, and do what is right by Him, then I shall lay no sickness upon you, for I am the Lord, your healer!

End of Scene V

Scene VI

In the desert

A cliff on the left.—The pillar of a cloud is visible.

> *(Moses is seen underneath a palm tree.)*

THE ISRAELITE: We hungered, and the Lord gave us manna and quail. . . . We thirst . . . yet you give us no water!

MOSES: Why do you wrangle with me? Why do you challenge the Lord?

THE ISRAELITE: And why did you take us out of Egypt: to let us, our children and our cattle die of thirst? Where is Canaan—where is the promised land? You know the way—it is the path straight ahead—yet you lead us upon devious roads.

MOSES: Do you know the ways of the Lord, you fool? Is He not leading us Himself—during the plight of day by a pillar of a cloud; at the dark of night by a pillar of fire?

THE ISRAELITE: We are the children of mortals—we are consumed by thirst—give us water! If not—you will die!

MOSES   (*Rises*): Lord, what am I to do with this people? They are not far from stoning me to death!

THE VOICE: You shall strike the rock—and water will flow from it. . . .

MOSES   (*Strikes the rock and water comes pouring forth*): Israelite, go and tell your brethren that the Lord has given you water from the mountainside—He, the Lord Who took us by His mighty hand and led us out of Egypt—out of the house of bondage!

End of Scene VI

Scene VII

The setting is the same as in the preceding scene.

MOSES: The Amalekites are attacking us. . . . Go, Joshua, and strike them down!

JOSHUA: How can I?

MOSES: The Lord is waging war for Israel—go!

JOSHUA: Your lowly servant does your bidding!

(*He goes.*)

....

AARON: Our time is running out—the Amalekites are attacking us in droves, like locusts! We shall never behold Canaan. . . .

MOSES: You fainthearted unbeliever!—Who destroyed Pharaoh's army in the Red Sea—who brought us out of the Egyptian bondage? The Lord is our warrior—His name is the Lord! He sank Pharaoh's chariots in the sea, and with them his power. . . . They sank to the bottom like rocks, and the water is deep above them!

AARON: The Amalekites are upon us—I can hear their warriors' cries!

HUR: The Amalekites are upon us—I see our men giving way—they are falling like straw!

MOSES   (*With outstretched arms*):   What do you see now, Aaron?

AARON: I see our men gaining the victory!

HUR: The Amalekites are turning back!

MOSES   (*Lets his arms fall*):   What do you see, Aaron?

AARON: I see our men giving way—they are falling—falling like straw!

MOSES   (*Raising his arms again*): What do you see now, Aaron?

AARON: Our men are victorious!

MOSES: The Lord is with us, and the Lord God of Strength gives us the power of victory through His servant's feeble efforts. . . . O Lord, Your right hand is performing great miracles. . . . O Lord, Your right hand has defeated the enemy!

End of Scene VII

Scene VIII

The same setting.

(Moses is seated beneath the palm tree.)

JETHRO: I, Jethro, your father-in-law, am coming to you, to your wife, and to your two sons.

MOSES (*Rises and bows to Jethro*): Be welcome, father, and behold how the Lord has delivered our people from the land of the Egyptians. . . .

JETHRO: Blessed be the Lord Who has delivered you from the grip of Pharaoh! Now I know that the Lord is greater than all other gods!

MOSES: Come into my hut, father, and break bread with the elders. . . . Afterward we shall go and offer a burnt sacrifice to the Lord—and then you may advise me how best to get along with this hardheaded people. . . .

End of Scene VIII

Scene IX

Mount Sinai

MOSES: Speak, O Lord, Your servant hears You!

THE VOICE: This you shall say to the house of Jacob and proclaim to the children of Israel. . . . You have seen what I have done to the Egyptians and how I have carried you on eagle wings and taken you to my bosom. If you now hear my voice and keep my covenants, you shall be my chosen ones before all other nations—for the whole of the earth is mine. And to me you shall be a spiritual kingdom and a consecrated people.

These are the words you shall proclaim to the children of Israel!

....

MOSES (*Calls outside*): Did you hear, my people, what the Lord spoke to you?

THE PEOPLE: All that the Lord has spoken, we will do!

....

THE VOICE: Behold, I shall come to you on a heavy cloud that the people may hear my words and believe you. Go out to the people and sanctify them this day and to-morrow and bid them wash their garments; for on the third day the Lord shall descend upon the mountain of Sinai. And place signs among the people and tell them to guard against ascending the mountain—for he who does so shall die his death. . . .

....

Moses (*Calls outside*): Did you hear, my people, what the Lord spoke to you?

The People: All that the Lord has said we shall do!

End of Scene IX

Scene X

The setting is the same, but Sinai is now enclosed by a fence. The sky is a mass of clouds, and there is lightning. — The sound of trumpet blasts is heard.

THE VOICE: Warn the people not to come close to the Lord lest they behold His face and turn into dead men! And the priests who approach the Lord shall consecrate themselves lest they be smitten by the Lord!

MOSES: The people will not ascend Mount Sinai, Lord, for the signs You have bid to be placed round the mountain, have made it a holy place, O Lord!

THE VOICE: You alone shall ascend the mountain, but the priests and the people shall not ascend to the Lord lest He smite them!

End of Scene X

Scene XI

On the crest of Mt. Sinai, surrounded by clouds

(Moses is alone.)

THE VOICE: I am the Lord your God Who has led you out of the house of bondage in Egypt:
You shall have no other gods before me!

End of Scene XI

Scene XII

The scene is the same as the preceding one.

THE VOICE: You shall not distress or cause grief to a stranger, or oppress him, for you have yourselves been strangers in the land of Egypt. (*A trumpet blare is heard.*) You shall not cause distress to any widow, or to the fatherless, lest they cry out to me and I hear their cry so that I become incensed and in my wrath slay you with my sword.
(*Again a trumpet blare is heard.*)

When you lend my people money, you shall not be a usurer. —If you take your neighbor's overgarments in pawn, you shall return them to him before the sun has set; what is he to use for covering when he lies down at night? Should he call to me, I shall hear him with compassion.
(*Another trumpet blare.*)

You shall not believe in lies lest you give aid to the ungodly, and you become a false witness.
You shall not side with those who are in power, when they do evil; nor shall you favor the lowly when their cause is unjust. (*Trumpet blare.*)

You shall not revenge yourselves upon or retain ill will toward the children of your people! You shall love your neighbors as yourselves! (*Trumpet blare.*)

You shall be a holy people to me!
Behold, I am sending an angel before you who shall protect you upon the road. . . . Therefore keep in sight his face, listen to his voice, and do not anger or embitter him; for he shall not spare you when you commit a trespass.

....

THE VOICE: Ascend on high to the mountain crest and remain there that I may give you the tablets of stone that I have inscribed and which you shall teach them! I will live among the children of Israel and be their God!

(*Moses ascends into the clouds.*)

End of Scene XII

Scene XIII

Mount Sinai
(As in Scene IX)

The Israelite and Aaron are seen at the altar with the golden calf.

THE ISRAELITE: What has become of Moses? We have not seen him for forty days and forty nights!

AARON: He is up on the mountain, speaking with God.

THE ISRAELITE: With *his* God—with the God who promised us Canaan and who instead is leaving us to roam in the wilderness—without anything to eat—without water to drink. . . .

AARON: . . . but who *did* lead us out of the land of Egypt!

THE ISRAELITE: . . . the good land of Egypt where our meat pots were filled, where we had leak and cabbage, where we were serfs, it is true,—but what good is our freedom in the servitude and oppression of the desert, at the mercy of hunger and thirst?

AARON: My brother Moses is gone from us. . . . We have not seen him for more than a lunar month; his God has abandoned us. . . . We cannot be without gods—that is why I have made this golden calf, as you asked of me . . . for you wish to be able to *see* your god and be in touch with him yourselves! Very well, here he is! Try to induce him to help you—I will not urge him, for I am waiting for the Lord—the Lord who saved us from the house of bondage and who gave us the promise!

THE ISRAELITE: You may wait for the promise! We will not!   (*He speaks to the outside.*)

Hear me, Israel—you who are walking in the wilderness without holy men, without sanctuary! Here is your altar of sacrifice—now I am lighting the sacrifice!

(*The People rejoice vociferously as the sacrifice is lighted.*)

....

MOSES: (*Descending from the mountain, carrying the tablets of the commandments*): Aaron, Aaron—what have you let the people do to you that you have committed so grave a sin?

AARON: May the Lord stay His wrath!—You know that this is a wicked people. They said: "Make us gods that will keep us on the right path, for we know not what has happened to the man Moses who led us out of Egypt."

MOSES (*Erects the tablets of the commandments upon the mountain. The calf is plunged into the fire*): "You are a stubborn, hardheaded people," says the Lord God. "One day I shall come upon you with swiftness and destroy you!" But I answered and said: "Forgive them their transgressions! . . . If You will not—then erase me, also, from the book that You have inscribed. . . ."

Now come to me—each one who belongs to the Lord! Come here!   (*Aaron approaches together with the Levites.*)

MOSES: These are the words of the Lord God of Israel: May each and everyone bind his sword round his loins and then walk back and forth through the encampment, from one gate to the other, and slay each and everyone—be it brother, friend or neighbor—each one who has worshiped false gods!

And when you have slain the idol worshipers, I shall erect for you a sanctuary to God in the tabernacle of the Witness. There you may enter and ask the Lord, the Invisible One; but none shall see his countenance, for "No man who has beheld me, shall be among the living." . . . So says the Lord, the Lord!

End of Scene XIII

Scene XIV

The Sanctuary of the Tabernacle

The curtain before the holiest of the holy is drawn.
On the left stands the table for the sacrificial bread; on the
right is the candelabrum.
In the center of the sanctuary is the incense altar.
The wall coverings of the room are adorned with angels,
flowers, and fruits. The curtain is made of dark blue, dark
red, rosy red, and white cloth, with figures of angels woven
into the cloth.

MOSES: Why are you troubling me, Aaron?

AARON: The people are weeping in their huts—the whole encampment is grumbling.

MOSES: Then I will speak with the Lord once more!
—I will go into the abode of the Lord, into the holiest of the holy—but you shall remain here lest you die.
(*Moses draws aside the curtain and the holiest of the holy*
becomes visible, with the ark and the two angels above it.
Between the angels, a flaming, fiery sky.)

MOSES: Why do You make Your servant sad, O Lord?
And why do I not find grace before Your eyes—why do You put all the burdens of our people upon me? Did I beget them, bring them into the world that You should say to me: "Carry them upon your arms as a wet nurse carries the infant, into the land that You promised their ancestors?" From where shall I take the meat to feed the people? They come to me in tears and say: "Give us meat that we may endure!" I alone can not keep all these men and women

alive; it is too heavy a burden for me. If it be Your will to reject me, then I would rather that You strike me down, hoping I may have found favor in Your eyes in other ways! . . .

THE VOICE: Gather seventy men of the elders of Israel unto me that I may take of the spirit I have bestowed upon you and give unto them, that they may help you to carry the burden so that you will not have to carry it alone. And you shall say unto the people: "Sanctify yourselves against tomorrow, and you shall eat meat—for you have wept in the ears of the Lord."

And now you shall know that the Lord your God is a God, a faithful God, and that He will be true to the covenant He has made with you, and have compassion upon all those who love Him with all their heart.

He will love you and bless you and multiply you; He will bless the fruit of your body and the fruit of your land, your corn, your wine, and your oil. Blessed be the people of Israel above all people!—Go now and send forth men to spy out the land of Canaan, which I shall give unto the children of Israel. . . .

Now go in peace. . . .

MOSES (*Moses closes the curtain. To Aaron*): God is a faithful God, and he is charitable. —

Summon the elders among you to me and let them wait outside the fore-court!   (*Aaron leaves.*)

MOSES: Lord! O Lord! Do not destroy Your people and the heritage You have given unto them! Remember Your servants Abraham, Isaac, and Jacob! Do not look upon our people's obduracy too harshly lest the Egyptians say: "The Lord could not lead them unto the land that He had promised them!"—For they are Your people and Your heritage! . . .

AARON: The elders are waiting outside. . . .

MOSES: Step aside—and let them remain where they are lest they profane the tabernacle of the Lord's Witness!

(*Aaron goes out.*)

MOSES (*Speaks in the direction of the fore-court*): You men of Israel, choose among you twelve commendable men to explore the land of Canaan. Let them go up by the south and ascend the mountains, let them see what kind of land it is, what the people are like that dwell therein, if it be a good land or a bad land, great or little, if it be fat or lean, what manner of cities it has and whether they are defended by walls or not. . . . Bring back with you some of the fruits that grow there. . . . And be of good courage: do not fret, and have no fear of the people there, for the Lord, your God, is with you—the great and terrible God. He, the Lord your God, shall in time destroy these peoples for you, the one after the other. . . . Now go in peace!

End of Scene XIV

Scene XV

The Fore-court of the Tabernacle

The altar, with the vessel of copper for burning sacrifices, is visible.

MOSES: The scouts have returned from the land of Canaan! Let them enter!   (*Aaron gives a sign.*)

....

(*Joshua enters with Caleb, bearing a rod on which are hung some of the fruits of Canaan: a large cluster of grapes, pomegranates, and figs.*)

MOSES: Speak, Joshua!

JOSHUA: We have explored the land from the desert of Zin all the way to Hamath. We came in from southward and journeyed to Hebron, and then to the brook Eshcol. We were in the land of Canaan where milk and honey flow; and these are some of its fruits.

MOSES: Caleb! You speak! How did the people of Canaan seem to you?

CALEB: Let us set off for that land and take possession of it! . . . To conquer the people there would not require too much effort.

MOSES: Your wish shall be granted! We shall take off for Canaan's land!

THE PEOPLE (*Outside*): To Canaan! To Canaan! The blessed land that has been promised us!

....

(*The Ten Other Scouts enter.*)

MOSES: What do you wish? What have you to witness?

FIRST SCOUT: We have not the strength to battle that people. They would overpower us.

JOSHUA: Your lips speak a lie!

SECOND SCOUT: The land that we explored draws the pith out of the inhabitants. It is barren and stony.

JOSHUA: You speak lies! That land is a fat land. Just look—look and see the fruits that grow there. . . .

THIRD SCOUT: The people we saw in that land were kin to giants—and we were as grasshoppers by comparison. Do not set out for that land!

THE PEOPLE (*Outside*): Do not set out for that land lest we be destroyed!

JOSHUA: Why do you defile that land?

FOURTH SCOUT: Oh, if we had only perished in the land of Egypt! If we would only die in the desert!

FIFTH SCOUT: Why is the Lord leading us unto that land?—We shall fall by the sword, and our wives and children will be violated!

SIXTH SCOUT: Would it not be better for us to return to Egypt?

SEVENTH SCOUT: Let us elect someone to lead us and start back for Egypt again!

(*Joshua and Caleb tear their garments.*)

JOSHUA: Do not abandon the Lord, and have no fear of the people of that land . . . for we shall devour them like bread. . . . The Lord is with us—you have nothing to fear!

....

MOSES: Give way, all you people! The glory of the Lord is shining upon the Tabernacle of the Witness! Give way—for the Lord wishes to speak to His servant!

....

(All except Moses leave. The pillar of a cloud appears in the doorway of the tabernacle.)

THE VOICE: How long will this people revile me? I shall smite them with pestilence and destroy them!

MOSES: Lord, You are patient and have great charity. You forgive misdeeds and trespasses—yet You let no one go unpunished. Therefore be now merciful in Your great compassion!

THE VOICE: I have forgiven the people but, as true as I live, the world shall be full of the glory of God. For none of these *(He indicates the rebellious ones)* shall see the land of promise—and none of those who have profaned me shall see it! But Joshua and Caleb shall see it!—I shall drag the bodies of those who failed to heed my voice, about in the desert; but their children I shall lead unto the land that you have disowned! As true as I am living! So says the Lord, the Lord!

(Moses alone. He is troubled.)

AARON   *(Enters)*: The Lord has struck down the ten scouts with the plague—the ten who profaned the promised land! And all Israel is weeping! . . .

MOSES: This hardheaded people that would not listen to His voice—that refuses the land that was promised them —now that it is given them!—Woe to us!—We were within sight of Canaan, but now the Lord has taken it from us! . . .

AARON: May we not enter it?

MOSES: Yes, *we* may! You and I, Joshua and Caleb! But not the others—although their children shall. . . .

AARON   *(Sobs)*: Woe unto us! Woe unto Israel!

MOSES: Now the trek across the desert begins!

End of Scene XV

Scene XVI

In the desert

KORAH: Moses has spoken and he has said: "You shall never possess the land but your children shall." Why do we drag our carcasses around in the sand—why do we walk upon our graves without either purpose or goal?

DATHAN: Do you call this the grace of God—to let us drift about like a flock of goats without a herder?

ABIRAM: The Lord has said: "You shall be a spiritual people"; and, behold, we are all priests!

....

MOSES   (*Enters*):   Why do you arrogate yourselves and why do you grumble?

KORAH: Why do you put yourselves above the Lord's congregation?—You are taking too much upon yourselves, you and Aaron; for all of us are sanctified, and the Lord is with us.

MOSES: The Lord has proclaimed who belongs to His flock, who is holy, and who shall sacrifice to Him.

DATHAN: Is it not enough that you have cheated us of the promised land and brought us to the desert to die? Shall you to boot be our Lord and rule us?

MOSES: Bring your censers and come up here!

ABIRAM: No—we will not!

MOSES: You would then learn that the Lord has sent me. . . . If you should die the way all men die—then the Lord has not sent me. But if the Lord should decide to do otherwise here, and the earth should open up and swallow you, together with all your possessions—so that you disappear alive into hell—then you will understand that Korah, Dathan, and Abiram have profaned the Lord!

End of Scene XVI

Scene XVII

(The earth is rent. Korah, Dathan and Abiram are swallowed by flames of fire.)

MOSES: Do you now see that I am your Lord?

THE VOICE: I am the Lord!

MOSES *(Covers his face)*: Woe be to me! I have sinned! Woe to me!

....

The setting remains the same.

AARON: The enemy is over us again, and the people are grumbling for lack of water!

MOSES: I would that this people were so far beneath the earth as Korah and his seed! I would that I were dead!

AARON: The Lord has abandoned us!

MOSES: He has in truth abandoned us. . . . He did so long ago!

AARON: Let us seek another God!

....

THE VOICE: Forget not your God who led you out of the house of slavery!

MOSES: To be driven out into the wilderness and having to thirst to death!

THE VOICE: Moses! Take your staff and strike the mountain rock!

MOSES: What good would that do?

THE VOICE: That you may have water to drink!

MOSES: I have no faith in that!

THE VOICE: Take your staff! The people are waiting below. . . . Let not your Lord and God be put to shame!

(*Moses takes his staff. He strikes the rock with his staff. No water appears.*)

MOSES: I do not believe! Help me in my unbelief, O Lord!

(*The People are grumbling below.*)

THE VOICE: Moses and Aaron! Because you were lacking in your faith in me and because you profaned me before all your people, you shall not lead this congregation into the land that was promised to them!

(*Moses and Aaron fall on their faces.*)
Strike the rock, Moses!

MOSES   (*Rises and strikes the rock. Water pours forth*): O Lord, You great, awesome God, have pity—have mercy on me!

End of Scene XVII

Scene XVIII

On top of a mountain in the desert

AARON: Where are you bringing me?

MOSES: Where the Lord bids me.

AARON: Why have you summoned my son Eleazar?

MOSES: At the Lord's bidding.

AARON: I am caught by agony . . . and I am in great fear. . . .

MOSES: Shed your priestly robe! And your sandals.

AARON: Am I to be sacrificed?

MOSES: Remove your headgear—and your headband and the ornaments!

AARON: Has there been a death?

MOSES: Take off the shield of office with the emblem of the twelve tribes!

AARON: Am I to be sacrificed?

MOSES: And the girdle!

AARON: Am I being rejected—condemned?

MOSES: You are to die!

AARON: Die?

MOSES: You have sinned! You sinned—as I did—when we wrangled by the waters of Kadish, for we did not believe and we were lacking in faith. You took part in the rebellion at Hazeroth; you made the golden calf for the people at Sinai. But the Lord forgave you and made your staff to grow green as a token that the priestly office would be handed down to your descendants.—You shall die! Eleazar, clothe yourself in your father's priestly robe!—My son, be like your father in his goodness, but abstain from his evilness!

AARON: The Lord gave and the Lord has taken away! Blessed be the name of the Lord!—Eleazar! Forget not the God of your ancestors—the God of mercy who brought you out of the Egyptian's land—out of the house of bondage!

(*He dies.*)

MOSES: May the Lord accompany your soul upon the unknown path, my brother!—Eleazar, let us continue the pilgrimage!

End of Scene XVIII

Scene XIX

In the desert

The serpent of brass is placed aloft.

THE ISRAELITE: We complained in the desert, we grumbled over our plight to the Lord. He heard our prayers, He gave us bread from heaven. . . . We complained about the bread—He sent us burning snakes for bread. Then Moses put up this serpent of brass, and we were given strength to live as long as we raised our eyes to him.

MOSES: That was the secret of the snake. Lift up your eyes to heaven—and you shall live!

(They leave. The snake disappears.)

. . . .

BALAAM *(Enters)*: Balak, the king of the Moabites, came to me, Balaam the soothsayer, and said: "The Moabites are agitated because of the children of Israel. The Israelites are gnawing at everything around them, much as cattle eat the grass. I want you, Balaam, to put a curse upon that people, for I know that whomever you bless, he will be blessed—and whomever you curse, he shall be cursed." . . . But then the Lord God came to me and said: "Do not put a curse on that people, for it is a blessed people! Now —how can I curse anyone to whom God gives His blessing? From the crest of the mountain I can see . . . and, behold, that people shall dwell alone and shall not be reckoned among the nations. Who can count the dust of Jacob and the number of the fourth part of Israel? You see that I have come here to bless. . . . I bless—for I cannot do otherwise.

This people shall rise up as a great lion and shall lift itself up as a young lion. . . .

These are my words—the words of Balaam, son of Beor — — — Balaam, whose eyes have been opened: I shall see Him, but not now. . . . I shall behold Him—but not nigh. . . . There shall come a star out of Jacob, and a Scepter shall rise out of Israel. . . .   (*He leaves.*)

End of Scene XIX

Scene XX

In the desert

MOSES: You have seen all that the Lord has done before your eyes in Egypt. He has let you wander in the desert; your raiment waxed not old upon you and is not torn, nor are your sandals worn out; but I have grown old and can no more go out and come in . . . also the Lord has said unto me: "You shall not go over this Jordan."—But you—when the time comes that you are ready to go over the Jordan into the promised land—you shall stand upon Mount Ebal and Mount Gerizim in the valley of Shechem. Those who shall stand on Mount Gerizim to bless the people shall be: Simeon, Levi, Judah and Issachar, Joseph and Benjamin.

(The six elders of these tribes place themselves on the right as Moses beckons to them with his hand.)

And these six shall stand upon Mount Ebal to curse, namely: Reuben, Gad, Asher, Zebulun, Dan, and Naphtali.

(The six elders of these tribes place themselves on the left when Moses gives them the sign.)

And as you are divided into two flocks, the way you are now, you on the right shall begin by reading the blessing I have handed down to you.

THE SIX ELDERS   *(On the right, they read from the table given them by Moses)*: Blessed shall you be in the city, and blessed shall you be in the field;
blessed shall be the fruit of your body, and the fruit of your ground;
blessed shall be your basket and your store;
the Lord shall cause your enemies that rise up against you

to be smitten before your face: they shall come out against
you one way, and flee before you seven ways;

the Lord shall command the blessing upon you and all the
work of your hand; you shall lend unto many nations, and
you shall not borrow;

and the Lord shall make you the head, and not the tail; and
you shall be above only, and you shall not be beneath—
if but you hearken unto the commandments of the Lord
your God, which I command you this day, to observe and
to do them.

THE PEOPLE (*Outside*): Amen.

THE SIX ELDERS (*On the left; they read*): But it shall
come to pass, if you will not hearken unto the voice of the
Lord your God, to observe to do all His commandments
and His statutes which I command you this day; that all
these curses shall come upon you and overtake you:

Cursed shall you be in the city, and cursed shall you be in
the field;

cursed shall be your basket and your store; cursed shall be
the fruit of your land;

cursed shall you be when you come in, and cursed shall you
be when you go out;

the Lord shall smite you with a consumption, and with a
fever, and with an inflammation, and with an extreme burning, and with the sword, and with blasting, and with mil-
dew;

and your heaven that is over your head shall be brass and
the earth that is under you shall be iron;

the Lord shall smite you with madness, and blindness, and
astonishment of heart; and you shall not prosper in your
ways; and you shall only be oppressed and spoiled ever-
more, and no man shall save you;

you shall betroth a wife, and another man shall lie with her;
you shall build a house, and you shall not dwell therein;

you shall plant a vineyard, and shall not gather the grapes thereof;

your sons and your daughters shall be given unto another people; you shall beget sons and daughters, but you shall not enjoy them, for they shall go into captivity; and you shall be only oppressed and crushed always;

the stranger that is within you shall get up above you very high, and you shall come down very low; he shall lend to you, and you shall not lend to him; moreover, all these curses shall come upon you, and shall pursue you and over-take you till you be destroyed—because you did not hearken unto the voice of the Lord your God, to keep his command-ments and his statutes which he commanded you!

THE PEOPLE (*Outside*): Amen. (*The elders leave.*)

....

(*Moses is alone.*)

THE VOICE: Behold, your days are nearing their end— your death is at hand! Summon Joshua that I may give him my commandments. . . . (*Moses does so; he gives a sign.*)
(*Joshua enters.*)

THE VOICE: Joshua, son of Nun! Be firm and strong, for you shall lead the children of Israel into the land which I have promised them . . . and I shall be with you!

....

MOSES (*Speaks to the people outside*): Take this book of laws, you people of Israel, and place it beside the ark of the covenant of the Lord that it may be there as a witness for Him against you! For I know your obstinacy and de-fiance; and throughout the days I have lived among you, you have taken no heed, have not listened to the voice of the Lord! . . . How much greater will your listlessness and indifference not be then after I am gone from you! . . .

Give ear, O you heavens, and I will speak; and hear, O earth, the words of my mouth. My doctrine shall drop as the rain, my speech shall distil as the dew, as the small rain upon the tender herb, and as the showers upon the grass;

because I will publish the name of the Lord: ascribe ye greatness unto our God.

He is the Rock. His work is perfect; for all His ways are judgment; a God of truth and without iniquity, just and right is He.

Do ye thus requite the Lord, O foolish people and unwise? Is not He your Father that has bought you? Has he not made you, and established you? Remember the days of old, consider the years of many generations. . . .

When the Most High divided to the nations their inheritance, when He separated the sons of Adam, He set the bounds of the people according to the number of the children of Israel. For the Lord's portion is His people; Jacob is the lot of his inheritance.

As an eagle stirs up her nest, flutters over her young, spreads abroad her wings, takes them, bears them on her wings; so the Lord alone did lead Israel—he alone.

But Israel waxed fat, and kicked: they provoked Him to jealousy with strange gods, with abominations provoked they Him to anger; they sacrificed to gods whom they knew not, to new gods that came newly up, whom your fathers feared not.

Of the Rock that begat you, you are unmindful, and you have forgotten God who created you;

and when the Lord saw it, He abhorred them!

O that they were wise, that they understood this, that they would consider their latter end! To me belongs vengeance, and recompense. See now that I, even I, am He, and there is no god with me: I kill, and I make alive: I wound, and I heal. For I lift up my hand to heaven and say, I live forever.

If I whet my glittering sword and make my arrows drunk
with blood, I will avenge the blood of my servants and will
render vengeance to my adversaries, and will be merciful
unto my land, and to my people, says the Lord.

THE VOICE: And now get you up into this mountain
Abarim, unto Mount Nebo, which is in the land of Moab
that is over against Jericho; and behold the land of Canaan,
which I give unto the children of Israel for a possession.
And die in the mount and be gathered unto your people,
because you trespassed against me and profaned me in the
midst of the children of Israel at the waters of Meribah-
Kadesh: yet you shall see the land before you: the land
which I gave unto the children of Israel!

MOSES   (*To Joshua*): Go in peace, and forget not the
words of the Lord: "Behold, I have bidden you: You shall
be firm as a rock and fearless!"

End of Scene XX

Scene XXI

On Mount Nebo

The land of Canaan is visible in the distance

(Moses is alone.)

THE VOICE: Behold! The land of Gilead, extending all the way unto Dan! And all of Naphtali, and the land of Ephraim, and Manasseh, and all the land of Judah unto the sea in the west; and the south with the plains of Jordan, and the valley of Jericho, the city of palm trees, all the way unto Zoar.

This is the land which I promised unto Abraham, unto Isaac, and unto Jacob, saying: I will give it to your seed, to the children of Israel, and you shall see it with your eyes—but you shall not go over there!

MOSES: O Lord, let now Your servant depart in peace —now that I have beheld Your glory!

(He dies.)

End of Scene XXI

HELLAS
(SOCRATES)

Persons in the Play:

PERICLES
PHIDIAS
EURIPIDES
SOCRATES
PLATO
ALCIBIADES
PROTAGORAS
CLEON
CARTAPHILUS
ANYTUS
ASPASIA
ARISTOPHANES
LUCILLUS
NICIAS
THE WIFE OF PERICLES
XANTHIPPE
THRASYBULUS
THEANO
KING AGIS
QUEEN TIMAEA
LYSANDER
TISSAPHERNES
CRITON
PHARNABAZUS
TIMANDRA
LAIS
Female Flute Players; Citizens of Athens.

The Settings:

Scene I: *A semicircular bench of marble at the foot of the Acropolis in Athens. At the apex of the Atheneum is seen the statue of Athena, illuminated by the setting sun*

Scene II: *The hall of festivities at Alcibiades'*

Scene III: *Pericles' house: at his son's deathbed*

Scene IV: *The hemicycle at the foot of the Acropolis*

Scene V: *The speaker's pedestal (Bema) at the Pnyx*

Scene VI: *The home of Socrates*

Scene VII: *At the home of Cartaphilus the Shoemaker*

Scene VIII: *The Speaker's pedestal at the Pnyx*

Scene IX: *In Aspasia's home*

Scene X: *At the Agora in Athens*

Scene XI: *Inside the abode of King Agis of Sparta*

Scene XII: *Within the abode of the Persian governor Tissaphernes*

Scene XIII: *The hemicycle at the foot of the Acropolis*

Scene XIV: *At the Pnyx*

Scene XV: *The ruins of the walls of Athens*

Scene XVI: *At the home of Aspasia*

Scene XVII: *In the abode of the Persian satrap Pharnabazus*

Scene XVIII: *Outside the Temple of the Unknown God in Athens*

Scene XIX: *In Socrates' prison cell*

Scene I

A semicircular bench of marble beneath the Acropolis in Athens. At the apex of the Atheneum is seen the statue of Athena, illuminated by the setting sun.
Seated in the half-circle are: Pericles, Phidias, Euripides, and Socrates. Plato stands behind Socrates. Alcibiades stands facing them. Protagoras, the Sophist, is seated on a bucket.

ALCIBIADES: We have ended our celebration of the victory of Salamis—the victory that liberated us from the Barbarian, the Persian King. And now we are weary.

PERICLES: Yet not so weary that we have forgot that it is our friend Euripides' birthday—and he saw the light of day when the sun was still shining upon Salamis.

ALCIBIADES: He shall be toasted when we are seated at table, with our drinking cups, and have a roof over our heads.

PROTAGORAS: How do you know that our fortune lies in being free of the Persian King? How do you know that Salamis was a fortunate day for Hellas? Has not our great Aeschylus described compassionately that tragic day of the Persians in his lament:

"O Salamis, O how loathsome to me is your name!

And when I think upon you, Athens, I must sigh."

ALCIBIADES: For shame, for shame, you Sophist!

PROTAGORAS: I am not saying that the name of Salamis is loathsome. That is what Aeschylus says—and I am not Aeschylus, as you well know. Nor do I contend that our good fortune would lie in serving the King of the Persians.

I simply put the question—and he who questions makes no assertion! Am I not right, Socrates?

SOCRATES: An assertion can be direct or indirect. A question can be an indirect assertion, and Protagoras made an indirect assertion by his question.

ALCIBIADES: Excellent, Socrates!

PERICLES: Protagoras has thus made the assertion that the Athenians would be happier under the yoke of the Persian King. What shall we do with a man like that?

ALCIBIADES: Throw him in the well!

PROTAGORAS: I ask to be heard!

ALCIBIADES: By the rabble! Yes—there you always meet with support!

PERICLES: One does not use the word rabble if one is a democrat, Alcibiades! And one does not quote Aeschylus when Euripides is present, Protagoras! Since Phidias is here among us, it would be more appropriate to speak of his Parthenon and his Athena, whose *peplos* is now being gilded by the setting sun. Courtesy is the essence of social intercourse!

PROTAGORAS: If Phidias' statue of Athena has to borrow its gold from the sun, it would seem to indicate that the gold provided by the state was insufficient, and that consequently there would be a deficiency. Am I not right, Socrates?

SOCRATES: It would first have to be proved that the statue was in need of the sun's gold—but as this has not been proved, all talk of the insufficiency of gold is of no avail. Besides, one can not borrow gold from the sun—and what Protagoras says is, therefore, sheer nonsense, and he deserves no further answer!—If, on the other hand, Phidias would like to retort, he might ask: Having created the figure of Athena up there on the Parthenon, can I then say I have created Athena?

PHIDIAS: I have created her likeness.

SOCRATES: Quite right! You have made an image of her—but after what model?

PHIDIAS: From within me!

SOCRATES: From no external model then? You have not beheld the goddess with your eyes?

PHIDIAS: Not with external eyes!

SOCRATES: Does she exist, then, within or without your own self?

PHIDIAS: If I were sure no one would hear us, I would answer: She does not exist outside me—therefore she does not exist.

PERICLES: Beware! The gods of the State!

PHIDIAS: Help me, Protagoras! I can find no answer. . . .

PROTAGORAS: As far as I know, Zeus did not create man—Prometheus did that—but Zeus endowed the incomplete man with a sense of humility and justice.

EURIPIDES: Allow me to speak of both Zeus and Prometheus . . . and do not think me ungracious if I quote my great teacher Aeschylus when I speak of the gods.

PERICLES: Unless my eyes deceived me, I saw a pair of ass's ears protrude from behind the statue of Hermes over there—and those ears could belong to no one but the renowned tanner!

ALCIBIADES: Cleon!

EURIPIDES: I care nothing about the tanner—I have no fear of the gods of the State! These gods—they are doomed to fall—as our Aeschylus prophesied long ago. Does he not say in his "Prometheus" that the Olympian shall be overthrown by his own son who is to be born by a young woman? Does he not, Socrates?

SOCRATES: Quite true, he does. . . . "A son she will bear who will be stronger than the father." But who he will be, and when he will be born, he does not say.

EURIPIDES: Be that as it may, I think that Zeus is lying on his deathbed. . . .

PERICLES: Be silent! The gods of the State!—Cleon is listening!

ALCIBIADES: I think Athens is in its death throes. . . . While we have been celebrating the victory at Salamis, the Spartans have risen and are proceeding northward. Megaris, Locris, Boeotia, and Phocis have already gone over to their side.

PERICLES: What you tell us, Alcibiades, we know already; but for the moment we are enjoying an armistice and we have now floated three hundred ships! Do you mean that there is something more to tell, Socrates?

SOCRATES: I am not permitted to meddle in affairs of the state . . . but if Athens is in danger, I shall take up shield and helmet as I did once before. . . .

ALCIBIADES: . . . When you saved my life at Potidaea! You are as brave as you are wise, Socrates, and that is why I love you!

EURIPIDES: No—it is not in Sparta the danger lies. . . . It is not in Sparta—but here at home. . . . The demagogues have been raking in the muck and stirring it up until it stinks, and, to boot, the plague has come—at the *agora* and in Piraeus.

PROTAGORAS: The plague in Piraeus is undoubtedly the worst. They are dying there like flies!

ALCIBIADES: And to think that I have my best girls down by the harbor! My flute-players, who are to play at this evening's symposium at the statue of Hercules. . . . But none of us have any fear of death, have we, Socrates?

SOCRATES: No one is afraid—yet no one wants to die. . . . But if you could find some to take their place, so much the better for our enjoyment. Perhaps Phidias can help you out?

PHIDIAS: Yes—but the ones Alcibiades has, are better. . . . And Death at table is like spiced wine! So let them come!

PROTAGORAS: Euripides does not like girls. . . .

EURIPIDES: That's a lie! I don't like wives!

ALCIBIADES: Nor do I! Yes—other men's!

PROTAGORAS: When Alcibiades was younger, he took the men from their wives. Now he takes the wives from the men!

PERICLES: Let us go in to the banquet and wall in our conversation. . . . Walls have no ears!—Support me, Phidias, I am weary!

PLATO (*To Socrates*): Master, let me carry your mantle!

ALCIBIADES: That honor is mine, youth!

SOCRATES: *Was* yours—now it is Plato's: and he is the one who shall once overthrow Zeus! Remember his name! Plato! It is a name in jest—because of his broad forehead. His real name is Aristocles and he is a descendant of the last King Codros, who sacrificed his life in order to gain freedom for his people.—Plato was born a king!

EURIPIDES: And Alcibiades is of heroic ancestry, one of the Alcmaeonidae,—as is Pericles, his mother's brother! A gathering of nobles!

PERICLES: But Phidias traces his ancestry to the gods! That is higher still!

PROTAGORAS: I believe I am related to the Titans—that is the greatest of all! I said I believe I am—for we really know nothing about anything—and scarcely that much! Isn't that so, Socrates?

SOCRATES: I wonder whether you know what you are saying!

....

(*They all go out. Cleon, the tanner, and Cartaphilus, an Israelite shoemaker, enter.*)

CLEON: You heard everything they said, didn't you?

CARTAPHILUS: I did, indeed.

CLEON: Then you can testify. . . .

CARTAPHILUS: I cannot testify, because I am a stranger.

CLEON: But you heard, didn't you, how they blasphemed the gods of the State?

CARTHAPILUS: I am a Syrian and serve the one and only true god. Your gods are not mine!

CLEON: You are a Hebrew, then?

CARTHAPILUS: I am a true Israelite of Levi's tribe— my ancestors were in Egyptian bondage but were led into Syria or the Land of Canaan by Joshua. There we thrived under Solomon and David, our great kings. But two hundred years ago our city of Jerusalem was destroyed by the Babylonian Nebuchadnezzar and our people were taken into captivity and brought to Babylon. Later the Babylonian kingdom was conquered by the King of the Persians, and now their offspring is chafing under the descendants of your Xerxes of Salamis, whom we call Ahasuerus. It is true that Cyrus, the Persian king, has given the children of Israel their freedom; and our prophets Ezra and Nehemiah are in the throes of rebuilding the walls of Jerusalem. But your enemies are our enemies, and that is why I fled here over the rivers of Babylon and the hills of Canaan, to the land we call the Islands, where the sons of Japheth live.

CLEON: I have only a faint knowledge of what you tell me; yet I have heard your people praised as being true to the gods of their forefathers. . . .

CARTAPHILUS: God!

CLEON: You have only one god?

CARTAPHILUS: The one and only true one—the same unchanging one forever—He who created heaven and earth and who gave our people His promise. . . .

CLEON: Which promise?

CARTAPHILUS: That our people shall possess the earth.

CLEON: Well, I'll be damned!

CARTAPHILUS: Such is our faith, and it has kept us strong during our wanderings in the wilderness and in our years of captivity. . . .

CLEON: Are you willing to witness against these blasphemers of the gods?

CARTAPHILUS: No, Cleon!—Because you are worshipers of idols; and Socrates and his friends do not believe in your idols . . . and that is to their credit. Indeed, Socrates seems to me rather to worship the Eternal One, the Invisible One—whose name may not be spoken—and that is why I will not bear witness against him.

CLEON: So that is the way you feel? Well, leave in peace now—but take care!

CARTAPHILUS: The god of Abraham, Isaac, and Jacob shall protect me as long as I and my house observe His laws. (*He leaves.*)

....

(*Anytus enters.—A tanner and statesman, he is reading to himself from a speech "Athens or Sparta—that is the sum of the point at issue . . .".*)

CLEON: What are you reading, Anytus?

ANYTUS: A speech.

CLEON: So I heard. . . . Athens or Sparta? Rule by the people—or rule by the beasts! The people is Athens—they are the cultivating force, the producers, the balancing element; and, like gold, they can be found at the bottom. The beasts are the rich and the honored: they are the lightest in weight and float to the surface like chips of wood, or cork! Athens is government by the people, has been and always shall be. Sparta is ruled by cattle, by beasts. . . .

ANYTUS: You mean it is ruled by the few, don't you?

CLEON: No—I mean it is ruled by cattle! That Pericles, a man of riches, who boasts of his ancestry, should attain the ruling position—this, Anytus, shows that Athens is governed badly. How can he possibly know and sympathize with the people when he has never been down among them?—How can he get the right perspective of them from up above? He sits up there on his gable roof and looks down upon the Athenians as ants—but they are lions, with clipped claws and drawn teeth. We, Anytus, who were born down there, raised on tanbark, dog muck and filth, we understand our sweating brothers, we recognize them by their smell, so to speak. But like seeks like, and so Sparta has felt itself attracted to Athens, to Pericles and his cohorts. Pericles is sucking Sparta into his fold, and we will perish. Pericles is an aristocrat. . . .

ANYTUS: Pericles is sick!

CLEON: Is he sick?

ANYTUS: Yes, he has fever in his body. . . .

CLEON: You do not say? Perhaps he has the plague. . . .

ANYTUS: Perhaps. . . .

CLEON: And if anything should happen to Pericles? . . .

ANYTUS: Then Cleon, of course!

CLEON: Why not? A man of the people for the people! But no philosophers or comedians!—So-o, Pericles is sick? So-o? . . . Tell me—who is Nicias?

ANYTUS: He is a man of position who believes in oracles. . . .

CLEON: Do not tamper with the oracles! I do not believe in them, but a state requires homogeneity in everything in order to endure: in laws, customs, and religion. That is why I cling to the gods of the State and all that goes with it. . . .

ANYTUS: That is as it should be! I also hold to the gods of the State—as long as the people favor them.

CLEON: You mentioned that Nicias. . . .

ANYTUS: I am going to the baths. Come with me, and I shall tell you. . . .

CLEON: But Alcibiades—who is he?

ANYTUS: He is—the traitor Ephialtes, who is to show the King of the Persians the footpath to Thermopylae.

CLEON: The King of the Persians in the east, Sparta in the south. . . .

ANYTUS: Macedonia in the north. . . .

CLEON: And in the west, the new Rome. . . .

ANYTUS: And at all four points, danger! Woe to Athens!

CLEON: Woe to Hellas!   (*They depart.*)

End of Scene I

Scene II

The hall of festivities at Alcibiades'

Pericles, Aspasia, Socrates, Phidias, Protagoras, Euripides,
and Plato are seated at table. At one end of the table sits
a skeleton by itself.

PERICLES: The question—in all amity—is whether or not Euripides is a woman hater. Protagoras, you may speak.

PROTAGORAS: Our friend Euripides has been married twice and has had children—therefore he cannot be a woman hater, can he, Socrates?

SOCRATES: Euripides is in love with Aspasia, as we all are, and therefore he cannot be a woman hater. He loves —with Pericles' full approval—Aspasia's beauty of soul; and therefore cannot be a woman hater. There is not much we can say of Aspasia's body—and it does not concern us. . . . Is Aspasia beautiful, Phidias?

PHIDIAS: Aspasia is not beautiful, but her soul is both beautiful and good. Isn't it Pericles?

PERICLES: Aspasia is my friend and the mother of our child. Aspasia is wise, for she knows herself and she has good judgment. Aspasia fears the gods and has humility and a sense of justice. She has good sense, for she keeps silent when wise men speak. But Aspasia has also the faculty of making wise men speak wisely when she listens to them: she helps them give birth to thoughts—not like the midwife Socrates who merely releases the foetus; she offers up her body to help their souls.

PROTAGORAS: Aspasia is like our common Great Mother Cybele—she carries us at her breast. . . .

PHIDIAS: Aspasia is the casing of the zither without which no sound comes from our strings. . . .

SOCRATES: Aspasia is the mother of us all, but she is also the wet nurse who washes our newborn thoughts and wraps them in swaddling-clothes of beautiful veils. Aspasia receives our unclean children and returns them cleansed. Aspasia gives nothing—but by receiving she offers the giver an opportunity to give. Aspasia is the wife of Pericles, for she is his beloved and she also bears him children. That is something *my* beloved cannot do—or what do you say, Alcibiades?—Oh, he has not arrived yet! . . .

EURIPIDES: I was accused, and I am now acquitted, am I not, Aspasia?

ASPASIA: You have acquitted yourself!

EURIPIDES: Dear, dearest plaintiff . . . and I shall now be making my plea!

ASPASIA: With your own words, I shall accuse you now! So says Hippolytus—which is you!

"Why should you let such scum and offal as a woman,
O Zeus, inhabit earth beneath the shining sun?
No—if you meant to plant mankind throughout the
    world,
it should not have been done by means of woman.
Why should not man bring silver, gold, and copper
to your sanctuaries and so buy his offspring,
each one according to the value of his gift?
Then undisturbed could men live without women in
    their homes.
But now, no sooner have we brought into
    the house this evil,
than we are shorn of our possessions. . . .
Thus you can see what nuisance and abomination
woman is; and all too plain it can be seen

> why her own father, who gave life to her and brought
>   her up,
> gives gladly to her mate a dowry to be rid of her!" —

And now, Euripides, defend yourself!

EURIPIDES: If I were a Sophist like Protagoras, I would answer: That is what Hippolytus says—not I. But I am a writer of plays, and I speak through my offspring. . . . Very well—I said it and I meant it when I wrote it—and I mean it still! But nevertheless—I love to have a woman now and then, although I hate her sex. It is something I cannot explain, for I was never a pervert as was Alcibiades. Perhaps Socrates can explain it.

SOCRATES: Yes—a man can love a woman and at the same time hate her. There is nothing that is not given life by its opposites; love is born of hate, hate of love. I love the wholesome goodness, the mother instinct in my wife—but I hate the original sin in her. Thus I can love and hate her at the same time, since she is both good and evil! Do you not agree with me, Protagoras?

PROTAGORAS: Listen to Socrates—he talks like a Sophist! But black can not be white!

SOCRATES: Protagoras speaks like a fool! The salt in this saltcellar is white, isn't it? But when you turn out the lights, it becomes black, does it not? Thus salt is not white—not exclusively. Its whiteness depends upon the light. I rather think that salt is in itself black, for the absence of light is darkness; and darkness is at heart nothing, transmits nothing to the salt, and the salt absorbs no property to itself in the dark but remains on the contrary true to itself, its indigenous nature, and is therefore black!— But a thing can be both black and white. This eel, for instance, is black above and white underneath. And so—a thing can be both good and evil—loved and hated! Therefore Euripides is right when he holds that he both loves and hates woman. I would say that only he who has nothing but hate for woman is a woman hater. But Euripides loves woman also. Ergo, Euripides is no woman hater. What do you say to that, Aspasia?

ASPASIA: Wise Socrates! You acknowledge that Euripides hates woman. Therefore I should assume that he is a woman hater.

SOCRATES: No, my child! I admitted—and note this well—that Euripides both loved and hated woman. I love Alcibiades, but abhor and hate his lack of character. Now I ask my friends here: Do I hate Alcibiades?

ALL: No, certainly not!

ASPASIA: You wise Socrates! But how do you get along with your wife?

SOCRATES: The wise man does not speak of his wife!

PROTAGORAS: Nor about his weakness!

SOCRATES: You spoke the truth! We make sacrifices to the earth, but unwillingly; we enslave ourselves—but without any feeling of joy; we tolerate—but we do not love; we fulfill our duties to the State—but grudgingly. There is only one Aspasia—and she belongs to Pericles . . . the greatest woman and the greatest man.—Pericles is the greatest man in the State, just as Euripides is the greatest in the Theatre.

PROTAGORAS: Is Euripides greater than Aeschylus and Sophocles?

SOCRATES: He is, indeed. He is closer to us—he speaks *our* thoughts and not the thoughts of our forefathers. He does not cringe before Fate and the gods. He makes war on them. His art is deeper, richer, his feelings truer, his images more living than those of the old dramatists. All the evil things that have been said of Euripides are but black stupidity and black lies!—But I wish to speak of Pericles now. . . .

PERICLES: Hold on! At the Pnyx and the Agora—but not here, my friend! Not that I do not need a measure of encouragement when beset by false accusations! But we have gathered here to forget—not to bring back memories of the past. . . . And Socrates gives us our greatest pleasure when he speaks of the nobler things in life—and among those I do not count the Athenian State!—Ah—there comes Alcibiades with his retinue! More light, good youths!

(*Alcibiades enters. He is accompanied by Aristophanes and the Roman Lucillus. Female flute-players and Laïs follow them.*)

ALCIBIADES: Greetings! Here is our host! Here is Aristophanes, a coming comedian,—here is Lucillus the Roman —now living in exile as a former *decemvir* who had a hand in the *Virginia* affair. You have heard of the virgin who was abducted and assigned to a man against her will? The Romans have virgins—we have not. How about it, Laïs? This is one of the many Laïs who have posed for Phidias! . . . Do not be offended, Aspasia!—And then we have flute-players from Piraeus. . . . Whether they have the plague or not, I do not know—anyhow, what do I care? I am twenty years old and have accomplished nothing—so why keep on living?—Now Laïs will dance for us! Dance, Laïs! Music!

LAIS: Not for you—but for Phidias!

EURIPIDES: Let the dance wait! Pericles is in no mood for it—he is grave and pensive!

PERICLES: I am in truth sad! I am ill—life weighs heavily on me—and the end is not far off! The Man with the Scythe is becoming restless. . . .

ALCIBIADES: The skeleton is thirsty. I shall drink a toast to it. Who will outdrink me? Socrates is best at it— he swallows half a jug in one gulp.

SOCRATES: Not today—the wine has a sickly taste to

me.— (*To Pericles.*) We have evil eyes among us here tonight—that fellow Aristophanes is not our friend. . . . Do
you know him?

PERICLES: Well, in a measure. . . . He looks as if bent
on murdering us.

ALCIBIADES: I empty my cup to you, Skeleton!—This is
the way Athens looks at this moment! The flesh has been
gnawed away by the King of the Persians, by Sparta and
Cleon! The eyes have been torn out by their allies, the teeth
have been removed by the citizens. These citizens. . . . Aristophanes knows who they are—and it will not be long before he lampoons them! . . . I raise my cup to you, Skeleton!
—There is a host of silent men here this evening!—Am I
seeing right—the skeleton is moving! . . .

ALL   (*Horrorstricken*): Woe!

ALCIBIADES: He nods to Pericles!

PERICLES: Hush! The candles on the table are moving. . . .

PHIDIAS: The saltcellar also. . . .

PROTAGORAS: The table is giving way—what is happening?

EURIPIDES: And the divan is rocking. . . .

SOCRATES   (*Rises*): A god must be approaching! The
earth is shaking—and I hear. . . . Is it thunder?—No!—It is
an earthquake!

ALL   (*Get up on their feet*): No!

SOCRATES: Yes!—When I was five years old Sparta
was struck by a quake—twenty thousand persons lost their
lives and only six houses remained standing! That time it
was Sparta—now it is Athens!—Yes, my friends, a voice tells
me that our time is up—like that of little birds—before we
have reached old age. . . .

....

(Nicias enters.)

ALCIBIADES: Nicias! That is enough to sober me up! When the circumspect Nicias comes to attend a drinking feast—what can have happened?

NICIAS: Forgive me for disturbing you—but unbid guest is never welcome, and the tidings I bring. . . .

(A trembling of the earth causes the house to shake so that bowls and drinking cups jingle.)

ALCIBIADES: The gods of the underworld are toasting us with our own cups! I return the toast!

PERICLES: Let Nicias speak!

NICIAS: Pericles! Your friend, our friend, the glory of Athens and Hellas, Phidias—has been accused. . . .

(There is a murmur.)

PERICLES   *(To the guests)*: Keep silent!

NICIAS: Accused . . . oh, the shame of it—accused of having diverted gold from the statue of Pallas-Athena!

PERICLES: Phidias hides his face with his mantle—he blushes on behalf of Athens! We swear as one, do we not, that Phidias is innocent?

ALL: We do!

NICIAS: I also took an oath on it!

ALCIBIADES: It is a dishonor to Athens when one has to take an oath that Phidias is not a thief!

NICIAS: Pericles, your son Paralos is ill. . . .

PERICLES: With the plague? . . . Come with me, my beloved!

ASPASIA: He is not my son, but he is yours—and therefore I go with you. . . .

SOCRATES: The house is crumbling—friends are separated—all that is beautiful perishes—and what is coarse and crude and gross endures!

PROTAGORAS: And the gods are sleeping!

EURIPIDES: Or they have abandoned us. . . .

ALCIBIADES: The gods are dead . . . let us find new gods!

(*There is another tremor. All flee, except Socrates and Alcibiades.*)

....

SOCRATES: Phidias accused of stealing! Then may the house fall!

ALCIBIADES: May everything fall together—from Pindus to Caucasia! Then Prometheus will be set free and will give fire and warmth to a freezing mankind. . . . And Zeus will descend into Hades, Pallas will sell herself to youths in heat, Apollo will smash his lyre and start patching shoes instead. Then Ares will dismount his charger and become a sheepherder . . . and upon the wreckage of the glory of the earth will stand Alcibiades—he, and he alone—with a feeling of his self-sufficiency and his all-powerfulness . . . will stand there laughing!

End of Scene II

Scene III

Pericles' house: at his son's deathbed

PERICLES: Two sons the gods have taken from me. . . .
Is this sufficient as an act of atonement and sacrifice?

ASPASIA: What did you have to atone for?

PERICLES: One has to suffer for others—just as the individual has to sacrifice for the State. I have suffered for Athens! . . .

ASPASIA: Forgive me if my tears dry more quickly than yours: the knowledge that *our* son is alive gives me consolation.

PERICLES: Me also—yet less.

ASPASIA: Do you wish me to leave before your wife comes?

PERICLES: You must not leave me—I am ill.

ASPASIA: You have spoken of being ill a long time. Is it serious?

PERICLES: My soul is sick. . . . When the State bleeds, I feel the pain. . . . Here comes the mother of my dead son. . . .

....

THE WIFE OF PERICLES: I have come to bring a wreath of death for my son. In place of the obol in his mouth, he will take with him a kiss from his mother's lips. . . .

PERICLES: He died of the plague. . . . Beware—it may mean death to you!

THE WIFE OF PERICLES: My life has already been a slow death. . . . A speedier one would be more welcome.— Ask your friend to leave us. . . .

PERICLES: If she leaves, I follow her. . . .

THE WIFE OF PERICLES: So be it! And now the last bond has been severed—the ties that held us together. . . . Farewell!

PERICLES: Farewell, my wife! . . . (*To Aspasia.*) Give me your hand, my wife!

ASPASIA: Here is my hand!

THE WIFE OF PERICLES: We shall all meet in a future life, shall we not? . . . And then as friends—you—she—and he who went ahead to prepare the way for hearts which the narrow laws of life kept apart. . . . Farewell!

End of Scene III

Scene IV

The hemicycle at the foot of the Acropolis

PERICLES: Phidias has been acquitted of stealing but is imprisoned as a profaner.

SOCRATES: Phidias imprisoned?

PERICLES: He is charged with having sculptured an image of himself and of me on the shield of Pallas-Athena.

SOCRATES: The populace! The populace that hates all that is great! Anaxagoras in exile—because he was too wise! Aristides in exile—because he was too just! Themistocles, Pausanias. . . . Do you know what you did when you gave the power to the people?

PERICLES: It was only what was right and just. . . . It is true that I am falling for my own sword—but I fall with honor. I am dying on my feet—little by little—like Athens. Little did we think that we were adorning our city for its funeral. . . . How could we know that it was our own winding-sheet we were weaving? Or that it was our own dead-march our tragedy writers chanted? . . .

SOCRATES: Yes—Athens is dying—but of what?

PERICLES: Sparta?

SOCRATES: What is Sparta?

PERICLES: Sparta is Heracles—brute force—the bludgeon—the lion skin. We are too civilized, Socrates . . . we are the sons of Theseus, we Athenians. But Sparta is the Heraclides—the Dorians against the Ionians. Athens is being killed off by Sparta; but Hellas is the victim of—suicide! . . .

SOCRATES: I fear the gods have abandoned us!

PERICLES: I share your fear—but the divine, the god-

given shall survive! . . . Here is Nicias—bringing with him
bad news. . . .

....

NICIAS: Yes, Nicias, messenger of evil,—having just
come from the Agora!

PERICLES: What is the news?

NICIAS: The Assembly is seeking aid from the Macedonians. . . .

PERICLES: Why not from the King of the Persians?—
Well—in that case the end is not far off. Seeking help from
the enemy? From those barbarians, the Macedonians, who
are crouched above us like lions on a mountain?—Go, Nicias, and tell them that Pericles is dying! Yes, dying! And
plead with them to elect the worthiest among them as my
successor—not the one least worthy! . . . Go quickly, Nicias!

NICIAS: I am going—but I am first going to fetch a
physician!   (*He leaves.*)

PERICLES: No physician has a cure for me. . . .

....

PERICLES: Socrates, my friend . . . this is a dying man's
farewell. You were the wisest among us—but do not be
offended by what I say now: Do not set your goal for the
unattainable—and do not trick or deceive by using levity
and speciousness. Do not enlarge upon what is simple and
natural. If you should reply that you are anxious to see
things with both eyes, remember that he who takes aim
with his bow must close one eye, or he will see two targets.
You are not a sophist—but it is easy to get the name of being one. You are not a libertine—but you keep company
with some who are. You hate your city and your country,
and rightfully so—but you must be willing to give your life
for them, for that is your duty. You are contemptuous of
the populace—but you must have compassion with them.

I myself did not admire them, but I gave them their rights and I gave them justice—and that is why I am dying! Goodnight, Socrates. . . . I see only darkness before my eyes. You will close them and place the wreath upon my brow. . . . Now I go to sleep. . . . *If* I should awaken—*when* I awaken, I shall be on the other side—and then I shall send you a greeting, if the gods permit it. . . . Goodnight! . . .

SOCRATES: Pericles is dead. . . . Harken, Athenians—and weep!

End of Scene IV

Scene V

The Speaker's pedestal (Bema) at the Pnyx

(*Cleon is standing on the Bema. Nicias, Anytus and Alcibiades are seated below.*)

CLEON: Pericles is dead and Pericles is buried. We know that. Let him rest in peace with his virtues and his faults, for the enemy is in Sphacteria, and we must have a leader for our armies. And that is a matter that Pericles' ghost cannot do anything to help. Here behind us sit two prospects, both of them noble gentlemen. One bears the name of Nicias, because he never won a battle; the other one bears the name of Alcibiades—and we have all heard of his victories: at the drinking table and with women. His character, on the other hand, we do not know—but some day you will come to know him, Athenians, and he will show you what he is made of. Here we have heard proposed a host of men to lead our armies—strange to say, all high and mighty, and all of patrician birth. Athens—which has abjured kings and their equals—now has to fight royal Sparta and must live up to its traditions. It must go into the field under the command of a man of the people—under a man whom you can have faith in. We need no Pericles to put up statues and build temples for his own profit and glorification. Athens has had enough of such toys and playthings. But now we have need of a man who understands how to wage war—one with heart in his breast and head on his shoulders. Whom do you propose, men of Athens?

ALCIBIADES: Men of Athens, I propose Cleon the tanner—not because he is a tanner, for that is something else.

It is true that an army may be likened to an oxhide and Cleon to a knife—but Cleon possesses other attributes that are exactly like an army leader's: his last sally against Pericles and Phidias ended, as you well know, in a triumph—for Cleon. He showed a courage that never faltered and a common sense that invited respect. His strategy was by no means a lion's—but he won the battle nevertheless. And that is the main point. I propose that Cleon lead the armies in the field!

THE PEOPLE (*Outside. First they laugh, then they clamor*): Cleon is elected! Cleon!

CLEON: Athenians! I swear by all the gods that I have never aspired to be elected to this post, for I am no warrior or leader!

ALCIBIADES: Cleon is jesting and he is modest. I know that he is the greatest commander our armies could have. He himself is unaware of his merits for he has never taken part in any other battles than those in the People's assembly. I urge that he be elected. I demand that he fulfill his duty as a citizen—and if he attempts to shirk it, I shall bring him before the Council, now that our country is in danger.

THE PEOPLE: Cleon is elected! Cleon!

(*There is laughter.*)

CLEON: Athenians! Hear me! Do you want me to go to war—I who do not know what an army consists of. . . .

ALCIBIADES: There is nothing he does not know—he is a universal genius—he can govern a state and he is a judge of all art—he knows all about legal procedure and how to get the better of a Sophist—he can argue spiritual values with Socrates—he possesses every public virtue and every secret vice. . . .

THE PEOPLE (*Laugh*): Cleon is elected!

ALCIBIADES: Cleon is elected! The People of Athens

have spoken, and he has no other choice!—Now, Athenians,
—now Sparta is lost!

....

CLEON: (*Descends from the pedestal*): Anytus—I am
done for.

ANYTUS: I am afraid you are!

CLEON: I have not the faintest idea how to carry a
spear or what manner of arms a hoplite should bear. . . .
I am lost!

....

ALCIBIADES   (*To Nicias*): Now Cleon is dead as a dog!
You have Alcibiades to thank for that, Athenians. . . . And
afterward—afterward comes my turn!

End of Scene V

Scene VI

The home of Socrates

XANTHIPPE: What are you doing there?

SOCRATES: For old acquaintance's sake, I shall answer you—although I am not bound to answer: I am thinking—that's what I am doing.

XANTHIPPE: Is that an occupation for a man?

SOCRATES: It is indeed.

XANTHIPPE: I don't see that you have anything to show for it.

SOCRATES: When you were with child, the child was not visible either—but when it was born you could see it. And, above all, you could hear it! So you see how tasks that in the beginning cannot be seen, in time become visible. Therefore such matters are not to be looked down upon—least of all by those who believe only in what they see.

XANTHIPPE: Is it things like that you do when you are at Aspasia's?

SOCRATES: Such things, yes, and much more.

XANTHIPPE: You drink freely there, too.

SOCRATES: Yes—you get thirsty when you talk—and when you are thirsty, you drink.

XANTHIPPE: What is there about Aspasia to attract the men?

SOCRATES: She has certain attributes that are the essence of social intercourse, such as consideration for others, good taste, moderation, tact, discretion.

XANTHIPPE: That's intended as a reproach, isn't it?

SOCRATES: I said it in appreciation of Aspasia.

XANTHIPPE: Is she beautiful?

SOCRATES: No.

XANTHIPPE: Anytus says she is.

SOCRATES: Anytus prevaricates.—So you see the tanner Anytus, do you? He is Cleon's friend and my enemy.

XANTHIPPE: He is not my enemy.

SOCRATES: But he is mine! You always like my enemies and hate my friends. That does not bode well.

XANTHIPPE: Your friends are dissolute creatures.

SOCRATES: On the contrary. Pericles was the greatest of men, Phidias the best, Euripides the noblest, Plato the wisest, Alcibiades the most entertaining, Protagoras the keenest.

XANTHIPPE: And what about Aristophanes?

SOCRATES: He is my enemy. Why—I do not know, since our aims are identical. I assume you have heard of the comedy he has written about me?

XANTHIPPE: Anytus has told me.—Have you seen it?

SOCRATES: I went to see "The Clouds" yesterday.

XANTHIPPE: Did it amuse you? Was it witty?

SOCRATES: What did Anytus think?

XANTHIPPE: He made me laugh when he acted out some of the scenes. . . .

SOCRATES: Then it must have been amusing, or you would not have laughed.

XANTHIPPE: Didn't you laugh?

SOCRATES: Why, of course. If I had not, they would have called me stupid for not understanding a jest. You know that he has depicted me as a rascal and a fool. As I am neither, it was not to be taken seriously—and consequently it was nothing but mere nonsense and levity.

XANTHIPPE: You honestly think so? I think it was dead seriousness.

SOCRATES: If you laugh at what is serious—do you

shed tears when you see something funny? That is nothing short of insanity.

XANTHIPPE: Are you implying that I am crazy?

SOCRATES: Yes—if you imply that I am a rascal. The one thing hinges upon the other.

XANTHIPPE: Do you know that Cleon has gone to war and is in the field?

SOCRATES: Yes—to my astonishment I heard it.

XANTHIPPE: Astonishment? Then you think he will prove himself unfit for war?

SOCRATES: No—I make no predictions about his capacities as a warrior, for I have never seen him in the field. I was astonished at his election, just as he himself was, because it was totally unexpected. If he were to be victorious, I should be equally astonished—because *that* also would be unexpected.

XANTHIPPE: In other words, you expect him to be defeated?

SOCRATES: No—I am waiting to see how it ends—to see whether he wins or loses.

XANTHIPPE: You would be elated if he lost, would you not?

SOCRATES: I do not love Cleon, but as an Athenian by birth, I would mourn his defeat—and therefore not rejoice at Cleon's fall.

XANTHIPPE: You hate Cleon but do not wish for his destruction?

SOCRATES: For the sake of Athens—no!

XANTHIPPE: But on the other hand? . . .

SOCRATES: On the other hand, Cleon's suppression would be a blessing for the State, for he was unjust to Pericles, to Phidias—to all who accomplished something that was great and glorious!

XANTHIPPE: I see a visitor is coming to us. . . .

SOCRATES: It is Alcibiades. . . .

XANTHIPPE: That wretched creature! I should think you would be ashamed to have anything to do with him!

SOCRATES: He is a human being. His faults are great —but so are his virtues. And he is my friend. My enemies I prefer not to have as companions.

....

ALCIBIADES: Ha! Man and wife philosophizing together! A pleasure to see! Speaking of yesterday's comedy— that Aristophanes is an ass! If one is to kill off an enemy, one has to hit the target—but Aristophanes struck at the sky! To hit the target, yes!—Have you heard that Cleon has been defeated?

SOCRATES: What misfortune!

ALCIBIADES: A misfortune, you say? That the blackguard was stripped naked?

XANTHIPPE: I think you must be ill informed, Alcibiades. . . .

ALCIBIADES: No, by Zeus, but I wish I were—that is, I both wish and do not wish. . . .

SOCRATES: Silence—Anytus is coming. . . .

ALCIBIADES: Anytus the tanner? It is strange that the fate of Athens should be left in the hands of tanners!

SOCRATES: The fate of Athens? Who knows its fate?

ALCIBIADES: I do! I am the fate of Athens!

SOCRATES: Insolence!

ALCIBIADES: After Cleon—Alcibiades! Cleon is no more—but I am!

SOCRATES: And now we have Anytus here with us!

....

ANYTUS: I am looking for Alcibiades.

ALCIBIADES: Here I am.

ANYTUS: Need I prepare you for the honor that awaits you?

ALCIBIADES: No need for that!

ANYTUS: Well, then take to arms! You are to be the leader of the vanguard!

ALCIBIADES: The place for me!

ANYTUS: At the head of the triumphal procession that is to greet the conqueror Cleon at the harbor in Piraeus!

ALCIBIADES: Cleon has been victorious?

ANYTUS: You did not know?

ALCIBIADES: Did I. . . . Why, of course, that is why I came here—to give the tidings of his—victory!

XANTHIPPE: He lies!

ALCIBIADES: I spoke in jest!—And so—to Cleon's triumph!

ANYTUS: Does is not make you glad, Socrates?

SOCRATES: I rejoice that the enemy has been defeated!

ANYTUS: But not that the victory is Cleon's?

SOCRATES: Is it not the same thing?

XANTHIPPE: He does not rejoice—and he had no faith in Cleon.

SOCRATES: Dou you wish to make me out a liar?

XANTHIPPE: You said you did not expect it. . . .

SOCRATES: I said: unexpected by all—yet therefore not unwished for!

ANYTUS: I know you philosophers and your galloping mouthings! But—take care! Take care!—And now, Alcibiades, you illustrious and dazzling one, come with me to receive the despised Cleon—the savior of our fatherland!

(*He goes out. Socrates gets up as if to leave also.*)

XANTHIPPE: Where are you going?

SOCRATES: Out—away from here!

XANTHIPPE: Are you running away from me?

SOCRATES: Would you rather that I stay and give you a drubbing?

XANTHIPPE: Are you fleeing from me?

SOCRATES: Yes—as one flees from evil.   (*He leaves.*)

End of Scene VI

Scene VII

At the home of Cartaphilus, the shoemaker

CARTAPHILUS: You citizen of Rome—you are like me a stranger in this city. What is your opinion of this State and its government?

LUCILLUS: The conditions here resemble to a hair those in Rome. The whole of Roman history can be summed up in two words: patricians and plebeians.

CARTAPHILUS: Exactly as here, yes!

LUCILLUS: However, with that difference that Rome has a future—Hellas has none.

CARTAPHILUS: What do we know of Rome's future?

LUCILLUS: The Sibyl of Cumae has predicted that Rome shall one day possess the earth.

CARTAPHILUS: What is that you say? Rome? No—Israel has been given that promise.

LUCILLUS: I can't deny that—but so has Rome.

CARTAPHILUS: Only one promise exists, and one god.

LUCILLUS: Perhaps it is the same promise, and the same god. Perhaps Israel shall be victorious through Rome. . . .

CARTAPHILUS: Through the Messiah, the promised One, Israel shall be victorious.

LUCILLUS: When will your Messiah come?

CARTAPHILUS: In the fullness of time—when all is finished—when Zeus is dead!

LUCILLUS: Let us live to see that day! . . . I will be waiting. . . .

....

ARISTOPHANES (*Enters*): Have you a pair of low shoes. . . .

CARTAPHILUS: At your service, Aristophanes. . . .

ARISTOPHANES: They are to be used on the stage— ha ha! Well— if it is not Lucillus! . . . And of uncurried leather—not curried! Ha ha!

LUCILLUS: What can you be planning for us at the theater now?

ARISTOPHANES: Why—this time Cleon is to act and dance! And can you imagine—I cannot find anyone who dares to act that tanbark dog—and so I have to play the part myself! I shall act Cleon! Ha ha!

LUCILLUS: Where is the Great One at present?

ARISTOPHANES: On a new sally against Brasidas. When general Demosthenes won the battle of Sphacteria, Cleon was given the credit for it—and thinking himself a mighty warrior, he marched against Brasidas. The pot stays afloat as long as, et cetera! I should not be surprised if by this time it has started to leak! Behold, Alcibiades!

....

ALCIBIADES (*Passes by the door*): Greetings! Cleon has been defeated in the battle—Cleon has fled—now I have won my victory! On to the Pnyx!

....

CARTAPHILUS: Things move swiftly in this country—so swiftly—so swiftly. . . .

LUCILLUS: Close up your shop, and let us go to the Pnyx! Now you will see great happenings. . . .

ARISTOPHANES: And I will get a plot for a new comedy! The day for tragedies is past!

LUCILLUS: You may be right, Aristophanes. . . . Athens is not worth weeping for any longer . . . let us therefore laugh!

End of Scene VII

Scene VIII

The Speaker's pedestal at the Pnyx

ALCIBIADES: Athenians, Cleon is defeated—Cleon has
been killed. . . . I now place my undisputed talent at the
disposal of the State. You know my little faults—but now
you shall learn to know my great virtues. Harken, Athenians! Once upon a time Hellas possessed Asia Minor and
lifted its wings eastward. The King of the Persians took our
colonies, one after the other, and now he has reached
Thrace. Since we cannot go eastward, it remains for us to
go west toward the setting sun. You have heard vague talk
about the great State of Rome that keeps growing and growing . . . Long ago our country took that part of the Italian
peninsula which is called Tarentum and that most beautiful
of islands, Sicily. But the Romans have encircled our colonies. In the north the Romans have advanced into Gaul
and Germania; the Romans press on in the south. The Persian King who used to be our enemy, is now almost our
friend; and the danger today is not the Persians, but the
Romans. Let us therefore proceed to Italy—let us go to
Sicily—from Sicily we can eventually compete with the Romans for the possession of Hispania and the Pillars of Hercules.—In Sicily we possess the key to Egypt; with Sicily
conquered, we can, if need be, leave the sinking ship Hellas. . . . The world is great. . . . Why should we stay here
in this wilderness and get moldy? Our soil is sucked dry!
Let us open up new frontiers. . . . Hellas is a ship ready
for the scrapheap—let us build anew—let us go out into the
wide open spaces—let us follow the sun on its westward

course—it shall lead us! . . . Athenians, let us go to a new
land—to Sicily!

THE PEOPLE   (*Outside*): To Sicily!

NICIAS: Athenians! Harken to me! Do not go to Sicily!
The gods do not wish it!

THE PEOPLE: To Sicily! Down with Nicias!

ALCIBIADES: And so: to Sicily! It has been proposed
and it has been acted upon!

End of Scene VIII

Scene IX

In Aspasia's home

SOCRATES: I warned against the march on Sicily, the astronomer Meton cautioned against it, Nicias also—but it was of no avail, for Alcibiades had been given a favorable answer from the oracle at the Temple of Ammon.

ASPASIA: Do you believe in oracles, Socrates?

SOCRATES: I do and I do not. . . . I have my own *daimon* which gives me warning but which never incites—counsels but never orders. And this inner voice tells me that Hellas shall never conquer the world. . . .

ASPASIA: Shall Rome?

SOCRATES: Yes—but for another power. . . .

ASPASIA: You know that it was Pericles' great hope that we would be able to unite Hellas—to form a union of all the States—against the barbarians. . . .

SOCRATES: That was what Pericles hoped for—and it was a lofty hope . . . but the will of the gods is greater than any hope. . . . Alcibiades' dream of world dominion for Hellas, and his visionary awe of Rome, were also lofty thoughts —but the will of the gods is greater still. . . .

ASPASIA: What effect do you think Cleon's death will have on Athens?

SOCRATES: None! After Cleon will come Anytus! Cleon will live forever, for Cleon means *thought,* and thought is eternal.—Here comes Protagoras. . . .

ASPASIA: The Sophist! I do not care for him—he is a grinder who wears down whatever will power and steadfastness the people have. His broodings and speculations take away their judgment and independence.

SOCRATES: You are right in what you say and you speak with good sense, Aspasia.—If times were different, you would have been sitting on a tripod as a Pythoness and prophesying. Like the priestess, you do not realize, perhaps, what you are saying—but through you speaks a god!

ASPASIA: No, Socrates, I speak only your thoughts— only your thoughts!

....

PROTAGORAS: All Athens is mourning—all Hellas! Woe!

ASPASIA: What has happened?

PROTAGORAS: Phidias—whose memory shall live for-ever—has died—died in prison!

ASPASIA: Woe! Then he has been murdered!

PROTAGORAS: That is the rumor in the city!

SOCRATES: Phidias is dead, you say? No—Phidias lives!

PROTAGORAS: Can the dead live?

SOCRATES: You can not destroy Phidias' spirit—and as Phidias' spirit is immortal, how can he be dead?

PROTAGORAS: He was given the poison cup to empty.

SOCRATES: Did they poison him?

PROTAGORAS: So they say—and it may or may not be true. Yet he is dead!

ASPASIA: All men in Athens die while they are still young. . . . When will it be our turn? . . .

SOCRATES: When our turn comes.

ASPASIA: Each day a tragedy. . . .

SOCRATES: While Aristophanes keeps on laughing. . . . Tragedy in the city—but comedy on the stage! . . .

....

(*Lucillus enters.*)

SOCRATES: Behold the Roman—the future conqueror —of the world! What tidings do you bear?

LUCILLUS: I have come to warn Protagoras. . . .

PROTAGORAS: Me?

LUCILLUS: You have been exiled!

PROTAGORAS: Because of what?

LUCILLUS: Because of blasphemy. You have denied the gods of the State.

PROTAGORAS: Who is my accuser?

LUCILLUS: The Sycophant—who is invisible—and everywhere present. Hasten!

PROTAGORAS: Everything is probable—nothing is certain.

LUCILLUS: But one thing *is* certain: you have been banished.

PROTAGORAS: You are right—and this being so, my thoughts black out—as will all else on earth! Farewell, my friends, farewell to fatherland, to home and hearth! Farewell, Aspasia—Socrates—all of you, my friends. . . . Farewell!   (*He leaves.*)

....

ASPASIA: Will the Athenians miss Protagoras, I wonder?

SOCRATES: He has taught the Athenians to think—and not to take all things for granted. Doubt is the beginning of wisdom.

LUCILLUS: Aristophanes has murdered Protagoras, and he shall one day murder you, Socrates.

SOCRATES: He already has—and my wife has gloated over it—but I am still among the living.

ASPASIA: The wise man does not speak about his wife, Socrates.

SOCRATES: Yes—occasionally . . . when his cup is filled to overflowing!—Think of it, I slave for my worst enemy and feed her and house her—and she carries on a war against me—for which I have to pay the cost. . . . It is not an even battle—but the wise man, who is brave, tolerates it for the sake of his children.—Here comes Plato!

....

PLATO (*Enters*): Master, may I be permitted to speak?

SOCRATES: Young Plato has had his schooling. He has learned to listen and be silent. Now he may begin to speak.

PLATO: Alcibiades is being accused and has been re-called.

SOCRATES: What is he charged with?

PLATO: That he toppled all the statues of Hermes in Athens before he sallied forth.

SOCRATES: He could not have done that—it is too much for one man. . . .

PLATO: The charge is definite: destruction of the gods of the State!

SOCRATES: That the gods of the State have been over-thrown, I do not doubt; but that Alcibiades has done it—that I do not believe.

ASPASIA: The gods of the State! How many have not fallen because of them!

LUCILLUS: The gods of Hellas have been moved to Rome and have been given other names!

SOCRATES: There you put your finger on it!

....

EURIPIDES (*Enters*): Be greeted, Aspasia . . . and all of you. . . . I must be brief—Athens is no more! . . .

SOCRATES: Gone—with Pericles!

EURIPIDES: With Alcibiades! The Athenians have been slaughtered in Sicily—Alcibiades has fled to the enemy in Sparta!

SOCRATES: Then all is at an end!

EURIPIDES: Nicias has been executed!

ASPASIA: Then we must buy ourselves burial tombs in Ceramicus. . . .

SOCRATES: The road downhill is swift!

EURIPIDES: And to think that Alcibiades should come to such an end!

SOCRATES: Alcibiades is not dead.

End of Scene IX

Scene X

At the Agora in Athens

On the left, a temple.

ANYTUS: Alcibiades is in Sparta. The Spartans seek help from the King of the Persians. Nothing remains for us but to do the same.

THRASYBULUS: To seek help from Hellas' enemy—from the Persians—would be treason!

ANYTUS: Nothing else is left to us. . . .

THRASYBULUS: We have had a Thermopylae, a Salamis, and a Marathon in our past. . . .

ANYTUS: But this time we have Sparta; and the Spartans are now outside of Decelea.—If the Spartans can court the Persians, so can we!

THRASYBULUS: Court the King of the Persians!

ANYTUS: It is too late to be lamenting—the legates have already sailed. . . .

THRASYBULUS: Then we can never again celebrate the victory at Salamis! Now we may as well remove the statue of Athena from the Parthenon!—Look at my back—not at my face! I have not the courage to show it! I am ashamed!

(*He leaves.*)

....

ANYTUS (*Walks over to the portals of the temple*): Theano, priestess, come out!

(*Theano appears in the doorway.*)

ANYTUS: Have you pronounced the curse on Hellas' enemy, Alcibiades?

THEANO: No, my mission is alone to bless.

ANYTUS: Have the goddesses of Revenge ceased to administer justice?

THEANO: They have ceased to lend themselves to the revengefulness of the mortals.

ANYTUS: Did not Alcibiades betray his country?

THEANO: Alcibiades' country is Hellas—not Athens. Sparta is part of Hellas.

ANYTUS: Have even the gods become Sophists?

THEANO: The gods have lost their voice!

ANYTUS: In that case you may close the temple whenever you wish! . . .

End of Scene X

Scene XI

Inside the abode of King Agis of Sparta

AGIS: My friend, you must not partake of our frugal repast at the public table—you who are accustomed to the splendors of Athens.

ALCIBIADES: *I*, you say? It has ever been my custom to eat the simplest food—to go to sleep with the sun and to rise with the sun. . . . You have no idea how austere I am with myself.

AGIS: Since you say so, I must believe you—but in that case your reputation has slandered you.

ALCIBIADES: You know my reputation then, and you recall the incident of the statues of Hermes—which I did not mutilate—and which were my downfall?

AGIS: But tell me now: do you believe it is the will of the gods that Sparta shall conquer Athens?

ALCIBIADES: Assuredly, and as certain as it is that virtue triumphs over vice. Sparta is the essence of all that is virtuous and Athens the den of all vices.

AGIS: It is being said that all its men have given up women and turned to their own sex.

ALCIBIADES: That is how low they have sunk, and that is why they must be exterminated—rooted out of the earth.

AGIS: What you say convinces me that you are not what I had been given to think you were—and now I can offer you the command over our army with complete confidence. . . . Now we shall proceed to Athens! . . .

ALCIBIADES: I am ready!

AGIS: Without scruples—when you sally forth against your own and your forefathers' city? . . .

ALCIBIADES: I am a Hellene and not an Athenian—and Sparta is the capital of Hellas!

AGIS: You are a man made for greatness, Alcibiades! —I am going to see our strategist. . . . You shall begin the march this very evening! (*He goes.*)

ALCIBIADES: Go, my King! Alcibiades follows you!

. . . .

QUEEN TIMAEA (*Enters*): Hail to Alcibiades—my King!

ALCIBIADES: Queen—*my* Queen! Why do you call your servant king?

QUEEN TIMAEA: Because Sparta has paid you homage—because I bestow my favor upon you—because you are of heroic lineage. . . .

ALCIBIADES: King Agis the Second still lives!

QUEEN TIMAEA: He will not live long! Win your first victory—and Agis will be dead!

ALCIBIADES: Now—for the first time—life is beginning to smile on the sorely tried exile. . . . If you only knew the sorrows of my childhood, my youth with its sacrifices! Wine was not made for me—woman was not created for me; Bacchus I did not know—Aphrodite was not my goddess—the innocent Artemis and the wise Pallas guided me away from errors and delinquencies toward my goal—which was knowledge, wisdom, and glory! Timaea, my queen—when I shared your bed. . . .

QUEEN TIMAEA: Hush!

ALCIBIADES: Then I came to realize that beauty is greater than wisdom, and. . . .

QUEEN TIMAEA: Hush! Someone is listening. . . .

ALCIBIADES: Who is listening? . . .

. . . .

LYSANDER (*Enters*): I am Lysander—the strategist!

—Now I know you, Alcibiades. . . . I hold your head in one
hand—but in the other I hold the honor of Sparta! Therefore I say to you: Flee! Flee before I strangle you—flee before Sparta's honor has been compromised!

ALCIBIADES: You have heard wrong, Lysander!

LYSANDER: Flee! Do us the favor—flee! . . . Outside
stand fifty hoplites waiting to behead you.

ALCIBIADES: How many did you say? Fifty! Then I
shall flee. Had there been only thirty, I would have stayed!

QUEEN TIMAEA: Alcibiades!

ALCIBIADES: Farewell, my queen! I thought Sparta
was more broadminded! . . . This would never have happened in Athens!—Now I am going to the King of the Persians! The Persians are much more civilized and know what
is proper—and there I will be spared from having to eat
goose-giblet soup!

End of Scene XI

Scene XII

Within the abode of the Persian governor Tissaphernes

ALCIBIADES: Yes—my teacher Protagoras once taught me that everything is born of opposites. . . . Therefore, you see, I have room for all manner of opposites in my make-up. Sparta and Athens are both just as dear to me; in other words, just as odious. The one has its gods of the State; the other its goose-giblet soup!

TISSAPHERNES: You have a great heart, stranger. Is there room in it for Persia also?

ALCIBIADES: For the whole world!

TISSAPHERNES: How do you like my capital?

ALCIBIADES: I like all capitals. . . .

TISSAPHERNES: But for the moment you must like mine the best. . . .

ALCIBIADES: And I do!

TISSAPHERNES: And then you must also like my allies.

ALCIBIADES: Who at this moment is your ally?

TISSAPHERNES: Today it is Sparta!

ALCIBIADES: Very well—then be it Sparta!

TISSAPHERNES: But—if it were Athens tomorrow?!

ALCIBIADES: Then let it be Athens tomorrow!

TISSAPHERNES: Thank you!—Now I understand that Hellas must be at the brink of ruin!—So—the old Greece is so far gone, so decayed!—Then it is scarcely worth the effort!

ALCIBIADES: My teacher Protagoras taught that all things should be measured by their relations to human beings. Therefore I measure everything by myself. What is of value to me is what I prize.

TISSAPHERNES: Is it such things your prophets teach you? Then we have better teachers. Are you familiar with Zoroaster?

ALCIBIADES: In order to please you, I wish I had known him from the time I was born.

TISSAPHERNES: Yes—then you would have been able to differentiate between the good and the bad . . . between light and darkness—between Ormuzd and Ahriman. . . . And you would have been living with the hope of seeing the power of light gaining the victory—and of atonement for all through suffering!

ALCIBIADES: Well—I can always try it! Is it a large tome? I mean—has it many pages?

TISSAPHERNES: What is the name of *your* holy books?

ALCIBIADES: What do you mean by *holy*?

TISSAPHERNES: From where do you derive your religion—your knowledge of the gods?

ALCIBIADES: From Homer, I believe.

TISSAPHERNES: I have read Homer—but Homer is a book for children—full of adventures.—You do not mean to tell me that you believe that Zeus is the mightiest lord of the universe, do you?

ALCIBIADES: Why, of course he is.

TISSAPHERNES: But he is a perjurer and a pederast!

ALCIBIADES: Well—I can not help that!

TISSAPHERNES: Listen, my stranger friend and guest, there is nothing we two can undertake together or have in common. We do not serve the same gods. You speak of us as barbarians! But I can find no name that is low enough and infamous enough to apply to a people that worship images and the like!—Now listen to me! Outside is an Athenian emissary! Because the Athenians are as rotten to the core as you are, they have forgiven you and are only waiting for you to return, for the Spartans are outside the walls of Athens. Go back to Athens—there is where you belong! . . .

ALCIBIADES: To Athens? Never! I could never trust them!

TISSAPHERNES: And they do not trust you! So you are well matched! Go to Athens—and tell the Athenians that the Persians will have nothing to do with them! The grapevine is drawn to the healthy elm—but it stays away from the rotten cabbage head!

ALCIBIADES: Is the Athenian outside?

TISSAPHERNES: He is cringing on his knees outside, waiting to beg the traitor Alcibiades to be merciful, to implore him to become their lord and master. You are their man, the people's man, are you not?

ALCIBIADES: Why, certainly. . . .

TISSAPHERNES: Then you have to change your colors—for now the nobles are at the helm in Athens.

ALCIBIADES: I am a noble, am I not? The highest in the city!

TISSAPHERNES: Keep shifting like a weathervane—spin round like a pegtop—and look for a whip to lash yourself with!

ALCIBIADES: I must speak with the Athenian!

(*He goes out.*)

TISSAPHERNES: Yes—do that! Speak Athenian to him. He does not understand our language!

End of Scene XII

Scene XIII

The hemicycle at the foot of the Acropolis

SOCRATES: You have heard, Plato, have you not, that the Temple of Nemesis has been closed because the priestess Theano refused to place a curse on Alcibiades.

PLATO: That is what I heard, Master.

SOCRATES: Do you not find it beautiful that vengeance has ceased to be worshiped?

PLATO: Indeed it is gratifying—for when social intercourse results in a constant mass of wrongs and injustices, and when mankind becomes imprisoned by such a chain of wrongs—then the first mortal who does away with vengeance is also the greatest mortal, for he has severed the chain—he is a savior.

SOCRATES: You are right! But can you tell me the difference between revenge and punishment?

PLATO: I scarcely think I can—for all concepts flow over each other—much like a river and its tributaries . . . making it difficult to say just where the river originates.

SOCRATES: Then—how are we to differentiate between right and wrong?

PLATO: Through Zeus's immortal gifts to Prometheus' imperfect creations, through a sense of justice and humility.

SOCRATES: That is the conscience, or what I call *daimonion*. . . . But now let me ask you: Have human beings a conscience? Has Alcibiades a conscience?

PLATO: Alcibiades is lacking in conscience; that is why he is a miscreant.

SOCRATES: But what would you say about the Athenians then, who called him back?

PLATO: They are debased, too.

SOCRATES: Yes—the Athenians are evil. . . . That is why they will be destroyed. . . .

PLATO: Criton looks as if he had something on his mind. . . .

SOCRATES: Criton must be silent and listen for a while yet. He is still in the elementary class.—What is your opinion of Aristophanes, Plato?

PLATO: I feel vexed at his distorted representations. I do not think he is human.

SOCRATES: What makes you say that?

PLATO: Aristophanes attacks and ridicules the Sophists but is a Sophist himself. He flays the demagogues—and he himself is the worst among them; he defends the gods—but has no faith in them. Such tactics are so entirely unlike those of a human being that he must be *in*human.

SOCRATES: Or a fool! A fool ridicules everything—even himself!—I see Euripides coming here. . . .

....

(Euripides enters.)

SOCRATES: Welcome to the hemicycle, Euripides! Our group is getting smaller and smaller: Pericles, Protagoras, Phidias, Nicias, Alcibiades—they are already gone from us . . . and soon *we* shall be gone. . . .

EURIPIDES: I am going this very moment and have come to bid you farewell. . . .

SOCRATES: Where are you going?

EURIPIDES: To the north—to Macedonia. It is a new land, a goodly land and wholesome. Here Aristophanes has a hold on the people with his grin. . . . He has sneered and mocked me and my tragedies to the point of destruction.

SOCRATES: If you wait a while, I may go with you.

EURIPIDES: What is there to wait for?

SOCRATES: The return of Alcibiades—and the ruination of Athens. . . .

EURIPIDES: Then I shall wait.

SOCRATES: Over the ruins of Athens we shall march out into the world. . . .

EURIPIDES: Are you not an Athenian?

SOCRATES: I am a citizen of the world. My thoughts have no fatherland—my thoughts are I myself—*I* do not exist, only what I think will live! . . .

EURIPIDES: When Athens no longer exists, I shall cease to be an Athenian—not before!

SOCRATES: Then—let us wait!

....

THRASYBULUS   (*Enters*): Alcibiades has landed!

SOCRATES: No!

THRASYBULUS: The demagogues have fallen!

SOCRATES: No!

THRASYBULUS: The whole city is going to the Pnyx. . . .

SOCRATES: Then we shall go, too!

End of Scene XIII

Scene XIV

At the Pnyx

Alcibiades is on the Speaker's pedestal.

ALCIBIADES: Athenians—here you have your Alcibiades again—the same as ever—yet ever new. I left you and your city with great expectations and an honest will; but you recalled me and sentenced me to die upon a false accusation. The wrong was therefore on your side—but as a generous conqueror I forgive you. It is true that I am the same as when I left. . . . Yet I am not the same—no more than you nobles are like the rabble that sentenced me that day. Age and experience have taught me the difficult art of living life. And I think I can convince you that—from now on and thereafter, when the State has been given a government of competent, able men, and wise men—we can lead Athens back to its glorious place as the first State in Hellas. I swear by the gods to be loyal and faithful to you so long as you follow me! Are you willing?

THE PEOPLE (*Outside*): We are willing!

ALCIBIADES: With your consent I shall be your lord and master—but no one can be a ruler without obedient subjects. Sparta reigns supreme because it has a ruler. . . . Let us learn a lesson from Sparta. . . .

THE PEOPLE (*Outside*): Is he aiming for the crown?

ALCIBIADES: No—no crown for Athens—no other crown than the crown of citizenship. . . .

THE PEOPLE (*Outside*): Athens must have a king like Sparta!

ALCIBIADES: No! After Codur no more kings! Our

neighbor Rome has had no king since Tarquinius—it is only the Persians who have a king—and you know the Persians—I know the Persians and their country, where only slaves and tyrants thrive. . . .

THRASYBULUS: Athens wants no king—Athens wants a tyrant—and Athens will get one. . . .

THE PEOPLE (*Outside*): No tyrants! Down with Alcibiades!

ALCIBIADES: Athenians! I have refused the crown! Why do you call me a tyrant!

THE PEOPLE (*Outside*): You want to rule—and want us to obey! Down with Alcibiades!

ALCIBIADES: How easily a mob is swayed! How changeable you are!

THE PEOPLE (*Outside*): He reviles us!

ALCIBIADES: I did not revile you!

THE PEOPLE (*Outside*): He denies it! He lies! Down with him!

ALCIBIADES: If you will give me your obedience, I shall lead you to victory over Sparta!

THE PEOPLE (*Outside*): We will not obey you!

ALCIBIADES: Then . . . farewell—for the last time! You foolish people—you cursed city! Harken, Athenians! Lysander stands outside the gates! I can hear the trumpets blaring and the horses neighing! Farewell, Athens!

End of Scene XIV

Scene XV

The ruins of the walls of Athens

SOCRATES: On the ruins of the walls of Athens! We are now Spartans! We wished for no tyrant—and now we have thirty. . . .

EURIPIDES: There is no more Athens. . . .Now I am going north.

SOCRATES: You do right! The tyrants have forbidden your tragedies, have they not?

EURIPIDES: They have indeed!

SOCRATES: And as for me—do you know that they have forbidden me to teach?

EURIPIDES: But you have not been forbidden to speak, have you? No! Therefore you can teach—for you cannot speak without teaching. . . . Farewell, you wise, gentle man! The Oracle of Delphi has called you the wisest of them all. It may have been the last word she uttered, for the oracles have ceased to be. . . . Hellas is no more. . . . Why?

SOCRATES: You may well ask!—Has Zeus given life to the son who was to topple him? Has Zeus been overthrown? Has someone come to take his place?

EURIPIDES: Who knows? The people have brought in a new god whose name is Adonai or Adonis. He hails from the East and his name means Lord. Who is he, this new god?

SOCRATES: You know as much as I do! He is said to meet death and then to rise from the dead. But they have a goddess also. Have you heard of Cybele, the mother of the gods—a virgin who is now being worshiped in Rome, just as Vesta is being worshiped by Westphalian priests.

And in Rome it was believed that the enemy could not be ousted from the city until the mother of the gods had moved in. . . . What does it all mean?

EURIPIDES: There is so much that is new, and it is as muddled as wine in fermentation! . . . Here comes Aristophanes. . . . Farewell, my friend—for the last time in this life!—

SOCRATES: Farewell, you last one of the great!—Aristophanes beckons!—Why—he is weeping!

....

ARISTOPHANES (*Enters*): Euripides—do not go before I have spoken with you. . . .

EURIPIDES: Can you speak? I thought you could only grin!

ARISTOPHANES: I am weeping.

EURIPIDES: You must not get out of character!—Are these supposed to be tears?

ARISTOPHANES: Have pity upon a comrade in misfortune, Euripides! The tyrants have prohibited my plays. . . .

EURIPIDES: Socrates—shall I have pity upon my executioner?

SOCRATES: Can it be that the Temple of Nemesis has been opened again! . . .

EURIPIDES: Shall I have pity upon my executioner?

SOCRATES: Aristophanes was never unaffected and childlike before—now he is!—I feel sorry, Aristophanes, that you no longer can abuse and revile me. Perhaps you would want me to try to get your comedies put on again?—Aristophanes, I forgive you—but let us instead weep together over Athens!

EURIPIDES: For the last time: Farewell, my friend— farewell, my enemy! Farewell, Athens!

End of Scene XV

Scene XVI

At the home of Aspasia

SOCRATES: Alcibiades has again fled to Persia. . . .

ASPASIA: I am tired of Alcibiades.

SOCRATES: . . . And Euripides to Macedonia.

ASPASIA: Fled to escape the memory of their wives. . . .

SOCRATES: You have grown bitter.

ASPASIA: I am tired—tired of ruins—of everything. . . . The tyrants are murdering the citizens. . . .

SOCRATES: That is the vocation of tyrants.

ASPASIA: Will we have peace and quiet soon?

SOCRATES: In the tombs at Ceramicus. . . .

ASPASIA: I do not wish to die—I wish to live—but live in peace!

SOCRATES: To live is not an easy thing. . . .

ASPASIA: Yes—if one can live in peace and comfort.

SOCRATES: One never does.

ASPASIA: No—not when one has a wife like yours.

SOCRATES: My wife is undoubtedly as bad as they come. Had she not been married to a man of wisdom, she would have been murdered.

ASPASIA: Xanthippe betrays you with her gossip; and because she does not understand what you say, she gives a distorted picture of you and your philosophy.

SOCRATES: I know she does—but there is nothing I can do about it. . . .

ASPASIA: Why do you tolerate such degradation?

SOCRATES: Why flee from it? The only time one is justified in fleeing is when one is confronted by someone

who is more than one's match.—And—she cannot victimize
my soul. . . .

ASPASIA: You are prohibited at the peril of death to
lecture. That is of her doing.

SOCRATES: Should she be the cause of my death, she
will at the same time have given me liberation! . . . Aspasia,
I can hear that our friendship is on the wane. You are sur-
rounding yourself with new friends. You are a different
woman. Let me bid you farewell before Lysicles arrives. . . .

ASPASIA: Lysicles? Do you know him?

SOCRATES: Yes.—The whole city is talking about your
marriage. . . .

ASPASIA: To Lysicles, the cattle dealer?

SOCRATES: Yes. But that is your affair. It is not for me
to discuss.

ASPASIA: And you think that Pericles' memory should
have been better kept, do you?

SOCRATES: I should have liked to have seen Aspasia's
memory better protected . . . but having seen Athenians
bedeck themselves with wreaths of flowers to celebrate the
destruction of Athens, having seen Phidias die in prison and
Euripides go into exile—I. . . .

ASPASIA: And what will be Socrates' end?

SOCRATES: Not as Aspasia's. . . .

ASPASIA: The gods are making jest of us!

SOCRATES: They are, indeed.

ASPASIA: Farewell, Socrates . . . the wisest one. . . .

SOCRATES: The wise one—because he knew nothing!

End of Scene XVI

Scene XVII

In the abode of the Persian satrap Pharnabazuz

ALCIBIADES: Then you think, Timandra, that Cyrus is starting an uprising against his brother Artaxerxes for the purpose of capturing the Persian throne, do you?

TIMANDRA: I am certain of it—and just as certain that he has ten thousand Athenians under Xenophon with him.

ALCIBIADES: Do you think that Artaxerxes has been warned?

TIMANDRA: I know he has.

ALCIBIADES: Who could have forewarned him?

TIMANDRA: You.

ALCIBIADES: Does Cyrus know it?

TIMANDRA: Yes, he does.

ALCIBIADES: Who has betrayed me?

TIMANDRA: I have.

ALCIBIADES: Then I am lost.

TIMANDRA: Yes—you are.

ALCIBIADES: To think that I should fall because of a woman?

TIMANDRA: Could you have expected anything else?

ALCIBIADES: To tell the truth—no!—Is there no escape?

TIMANDRA: Not for you, but for me!

ALCIBIADES: I see smoke. . . . Is the house on fire?

TIMANDRA: The house is on fire; and outside are bowmen. . . .

ALCIBIADES: The comedy is over—the tragedy begins. . . .

TIMANDRA: And the play of satire commences. . . .

ALCIBIADES: My feet are feeling the heat . . . soon

Death will come with its freezing hands. . . .

TIMANDRA: Everything is given life by its opposite—
but here Alcibiades is dying. . . .

ALCIBIADES: Give me a kiss!

TIMANDRA: It is yours. . . .

ALCIBIADES: Thank you!

TIMANDRA: Go to the window and you will see something!

ALCIBIADES   (*Goes to the window*): I see. . . . (*He is
struck in the chest by an arrow.*) . . . Now I can see nothing!
It is getting dark. . . . And I had thought the light would
come. . . . Oh, Socrates! How little you knew! . . . (*He dies.*)

End of Scene XVII

Scene XVIII

Outside the Temple of the Unknown God in Athens

SOCRATES: This is the temple of the unknown god!
Who is this unknown god, Plato?

PLATO: Since he is unknown—how can anybody know
him?

SOCRATES: Criton may like to say something. Who
is this unknown god?

CRITON: He may be known to other peoples, though
he is unknown to us.

SOCRATES: You are right! What other peoples know
him?

LUCILLUS: The Romans also know the unknown god.

SOCRATES: Can the Romans know anything of the unknown?   .

LUCILLUS: They may have knowledge of his existence.
Is there a kinship between him and Zeus, and is he per-
chance the son who, it is said, is to cause the downfall of
Zeus—and whose coming Aeschylus has predicted?

PLATO: We know nothing about that. . . .

SOCRATES: Do the gods exist for our benefit alone—or
do they exist by and for themselves as well?

PLATO: The spiritual and the divine exist of themselves, but the gods derive their existence from us.

SOCRATES: If Anytus, who succeeded Cleon, heard you
say that, he would destroy us.

CRITON: Anytus has many ears—here comes *one* of
them!

SOCRATES: Oh no!—It is the Hebrew Cartaphilus. . . .
He is our friend, first and foremost!

....

(*Cartaphilus enters with his two sons.*)

SOCRATES: Tell us, man of the Hebrews, if you know the Unknown God?

CARTAPHILUS: I know only one God.—What does the prophet say, Esau?

ESAU: Have we not all *one* father? Has not *one* God created us?

SOCRATES: What is the name of your God?

CARTAPHILUS: His right name may not be spoken— but he is concealed under the name of Adonai.

SOCRATES: Is it Adonis, the new god who has been brought from the East?

CARTAPHILUS: I know only *one* God! Tell us, Jacob— who is He?

JACOB: He is the God of Abraham, Isaac, and Jacob, Who gave the promise to Abraham and Who brought our forefathers out of the Egyptian bondage.

SOCRATES: This is something I am in ignorance of— as ignorant as I am of the Unknown God!

....

ANYTUS (*Enters*): Socrates, you are corrupting our youth. . . . You are forbidden to teach—at the peril of being sentenced to death. . . . Even now, you are being prosecuted. . . .

SOCRATES: May the will of the gods be done!—Will I be permitted to speak in my defense?

ANYTUS: That you may! But the heliasts would prefer that you leave the country! . . .

SOCRATES: I will not flee!

ANYTUS: Then you will be imprisoned!

SOCRATES: So be it!

End of Scene XVIII

Scene XIX

In Socrates' prison cell

SOCRATES: Do not weep! You are not to blame for this.

XANTHIPPE: Would you not like to see the children?

SOCRATES: Why should I tear their little hearts asunder by saying good-by to them when it is not necessary? But you go home to the boys and console them. . . . Distract them with an outing in the woods. . . .

XANTHIPPE: Would you like us to be happy while you are dying?

SOCRATES: You should be glad that my suffering is at an end . . . you should be happy that I die with honor—for the fictitious crimes against fictitious gods that I have been accused of, they are nothing to be ashamed of—nothing but a plot in a stage play—where everything is make-believe. . . .

XANTHIPPE: Have you no final wish?

SOCRATES: I wish for nothing. . . . Yes, peace—escape from all your foolish sighs and tears and your annoying wailing and complaints! . . . Go, wife, and keep in mind that Socrates wishes to sleep—for he is worn-out and testy. . . . Bear in mind that he will waken again and then will be rested, rejuvenated, happy, and pleasant!

XANTHIPPE: I wish you had taught me all this long ago . . . for I had nothing that I could teach you. . . .

SOCRATES: Oh yes, my friend. . . . You taught me one thing—patience. . . .

XANTHIPPE: Can you forgive me?

SOCRATES: I cannot forgive you once more: I have already done so. Bid me farewell now—as if I were going

on a journey! . . . Say: Welcome back!—as if I were already
back. . . .

XANTHIPPE: Farewell, then, Socrates—and do not be
angry with me. . . .

SOCRATES: No—I am full of goodness!

XANTHIPPE: Farewell—forever, Socrates. . . .

SOCRATES: Not for ever! You wish me to come back,
don't you? Show a happy face and say: We shall see each
other again!

XANTHIPPE: We shall see each other again!

SOCRATES: There!—We shall see each other again!
And then we shall go—together with the children—out into
the woods. . . .

XANTHIPPE: You were not the man I thought you
were, Socrates. . . .

SOCRATES: Go now—or there will be no end to this. . . .

(*Xanthippe leaves.*)

. . . .

(*Plato and Criton enter.*)

SOCRATES: The moment is approaching, my friends. . . .

PLATO: Are you keeping up your calm, Master?

SOCRATES: To tell the truth, I am quite composed. I
would not say that I am filled with joy—but my conscience
tells me nothing that is disturbing.

PLATO: When shall it. . . . When, Socrates, shall it take
place?

SOCRATES: You mean—when shall I empty the cup?—
Plato—my best friend—my dear friend. . . . Time is short—
I have just come out of a sleep—I have been on the other
side. . . . For a fleeting moment I have seen the pristine
original of unblemished beauty . . . of which what we see
here on this earth is but a faded image. . . . I have beheld
the future—the fate of mankind. . . . I have spoken with the

high, the mighty, and the pure in spirit. . . . I have witnessed the wise orderliness that rules the vast, seemingly chaotic, disorder. . . . I have trembled at the thought of the unfathomable secrets of the universe, which I captured in a moment's divination . . . and I became conscious of the colossal vastness of my ignorance. . . . Plato—you shall write it down. . . . You shall teach humanity to look with sober restraint upon the things we see with our senses—to look up to the unseen with reverence—to pay homage to beauty —to cultivate virtue and to hope for our deliverance— through labor, sacrifices, and the performance of our duties. . . .

> (*He goes over to his bunk and lies down.*)

PLATO: Master—your are ill!

SOCRATES: No—I have been ailing, but now I am getting well—and would be prepared to make an offering to Aesculapius. . . .

CRITON (*To Plato*): He has emptied the potion cup. . . .

PLATO (*To Socrates*): You have already. . . .

SOCRATES: I have already emptied the cup.—Do not weep. . . .

PLATO: The wisest one leaves us—the most virtuous one. . . .

SOCRATES: Virtue is greater than wisdom. . . . I thank you for those words. . . . No mortal is wise—but I praise the gods for giving me humility—and a sense of justice. . . .

> (*There is silence.*)

PLATO: Socrates is dead!

End of Scene XIX

THE LAMB
AND
THE BEAST
(CHRIST)

Persons in the Play:

FIRST SHEPHERD
SECOND SHEPHERD
THE ANGEL
CASPAR
MELCHIOR } The three wise men
BALTHAZAR
MARY—with the child JESUS
CARTAPHILUS
LUCILLUS
JOSEPH
PILATE
PORCIA
SIMON PETER
HEROD THE TETRARCH
CAIPHAS
ANNAS
JUDAS ISCARIOT
JOHN THE EVANGELIST
PETER
ZACCHEUS
THE MAN with the pitcher of water
JACOB
THE SOLDIER
CALIGULA
THE PRIEST
CHAEREA
CLAUDIUS
CAIUS SILIUS
NARCISSUS
MESSALINA

PALLAS
GAIUS
ERASTUS
ALEXANDER
TIMOTHY
PHAON
FIRST SOLDIER
SECOND SOLDIER
THE SLAVE
People; soldiers; members of the Sanhedrin, etc.

The Settings:

Scene I: *Outside Bethlehem*

Scene II: *Outside the stable at Bethlehem*

Scene III: *Outside the Temple of the Sun at Leontopolis*

Scene IV: *Before the Roman governor Pontius Pilate*

Scene V: *The fore-court of the temple*

Scene VI: *Before the Great Sanhedrin*

Scene VII: *A street in Jerusalem*

Scene VIII: *At Gethsemane*

Scene IX: *At Pilate's*

Scene X: *Golgotha*

Scene XI: *The Temple of Jupiter Latiaris in Rome, showing the statue of Caligula as Jupiter*

Scene XII: *In the Palace of Emperor Claudius in Rome*

Scene XIII: *At the Court of Emperor Nero in Rome*

Scene XIV: *In the Catacombs*

Scene XV: *In front of Phaon's country home.*

PART I

Scene I

Outside Bethlehem

FIRST SHEPHERD: Tell me, neighbor, how far into the night are we come?

SECOND SHEPHERD: The second watch—the Dog Star is high above the horizon.

FIRST SHEPHERD: Were you in the city yesterday and registered for the tax?

SECOND SHEPHERD: I was. The pagan Romans have the audacity to take a census of the people. . . .

FIRST SHEPHERD: The Lord has brought to pass His punishment upon Israel. . . . We were in the Egyptian bondage—then we were prisoners in Babylon—and after that the Macedonians enslaved us—and now we are under the yoke of the Romans. . . .

SECOND SHEPHERD: And they want to impose strange gods upon us! Caesar Augustus has had a temple erected to himself, where he is being worshiped! How much further can the abomination go? Has the Lord completely forgotten the promise that He gave our Father Abraham?

FIRST SHEPHERD: The Jews are enchained in misery and in bitter slavery—they are surrounded by pagans, and can find neither rest nor peace—all their persecutors inflict their wickedness upon them.

SECOND SHEPHERD: The roads to Zion are laid waste and all the gates are deserted. Their high priests grieve with misgiving, their maidens look piteous, and every Jew is lamenting.

FIRST SHEPHERD (*In supplication to the heavens*):
Have You disowned Judah, or has Your soul a loathing for
Zion? Why have You thus struck us that there can be no
recovery? We had hoped we were to have peace; but we
can see nothing but evil coming of this. . . .

SECOND SHEPHERD: Behold, neighbor,—that streak of
light there! Is it the moon coming up?

FIRST SHEPHERD: Woe to us—it is coming toward us!
It is not the moon. . . .

SECOND SHEPHERD: It is either a pillar of light or a
specter! . . .

FIRST SHEPHERD: God help us!

....

THE ANGEL (*Enters surrounded by a shining light*):
Fear not, for, behold, I bring you good tidings of great joy,
which shall be to all people. For unto you is born this day
in the city of David a Saviour which is Christ the Lord. . . .

(*The Angel disappears.*)

CHORUS OF ANGELS (*From above*):
Glory to God in the highest—
On earth peace —
And good will toward men!

....

(*The Three Wise Men, Caspar, Melchior, and Balthazar
enter.*)

CASPAR: Where is he that is born King of the Jews?
We have seen his star in the east and have come to worship
him.

FIRST SHEPHERD: Arise, shine, Jerusalem, for your
light is come and the glory of the Lord is risen upon you,
for, behold, the darkness shall cover the earth and gross
darkness the people. But the Lord shall arise upon you, and
His glory shall be seen upon you!

SECOND SHEPHERD: Rejoice, O heavens,—be joyful, O earth,—break forth into singing, O mountains! For the Lord has comforted His people, and will have mercy upon His afflicted.

FIRST SHEPHERD: Let us go to Bethlehem and see what has come to pass—what the Lord has done for us. . . .

End of Scene I

Scene II

Outside the stable at Bethlehem

MELCHIOR: When Herod the king heard the tidings of the birth of the King of the Jews, he inquired of us where he was born. In the words of the Prophet we answered him: "In Bethlehem.—You, Bethlehem, in the land of Judah are by no means the least of the cities of that land—for from you shall come the King who shall be the Lord of my people of Israel."—This frightened Herod, and he said to us: "Go and search diligently for the child, and when you have found him, come and tell me."—But the Angel of the Lord appeared to us in a dream and warned us not to return to Herod, saying he would slay the young child. . . .

....

(*Mary appears in the doorway with the child.*)

BALTHAZAR: Hail, Mary, blessed be you among women and blessed be the fruit of your womb.

MARY: In my soul I praise the Lord, and my spirit rejoices in God, for He has seen the lowliness of His servant: The Almighty has performed great things through me, and His name is holy; His compassion endures from generation to generation upon those who hold Him in awe.

FIRST SHEPHERD: "This day a light shall shine, for unto us is born a Lord, and He shall be named The Mighty God, Wonderful, The Prince of Peace, The everlasting Father, and His kingdom shall have no end!"

End of Scene II

Scene III

Outside the Temple of the Sun at Leontopolis

CARTAPHILUS: Wanderer, could you tell me the way to the City of the Sun?

LUCILLUS: You see it before you.

CARTAPHILUS: This is Beth Semes, is it not?

LUCILLUS: This is Heliopolis—where Greeks and Romans have obtained knowledge and wisdom. Plato himself dwelt here once. . . .

CARTAPHILUS: This is the land of Goshen that our Father Abraham visited and that was given to Jacob. Israel wandered into Canaan, but after Nebuchadnezzar had destroyed Jerusalem, their descendants came back here and brought our people into the Babylonian captivity. Are there many Hebrews here?

LUCILLUS: Many thousands—and they have been allowed to build their own temple.

CARTAPHILUS: Then this is a Roman land, is it?

LUCILLUS: Yes.

CARTAPHILUS: The Romans are the rulers everywhere today: Syria is Roman—so is our own Canaan—Greece—Egypt. . . .

LUCILLUS: Germania — Gaul — Britannia — the whole world belongs to the Romans, as the Sibylline Books prophesied.

CARTAPHILUS: But the world shall be saved through Israel—according to the promise God Himself gave to our Father Abraham.

LUCILLUS: I have heard that fable before—but for the moment it is Rome that holds that promise in her hand.— Do you come from Jerusalem?

CARTAPHILUS: I come from the desert and with me are my wife and child. The child I saved from the clutches of Herod. . . .

LUCILLUS: Herod the Tetrarch—yes, what is it I have heard of him . . . there is a rumor. . . .

CARTAPHILUS: Wise men from the east had prophesied that a child was to be born in Bethlehem and was to be the King of the Jews . . . and therefore Herod ordered all male infants in that area to be put to death—just as Pharaoh once killed off all our first-born in Egypt.

LUCILLUS: The King of the Jews? Who could that be?

CARTAPHILUS: Messiah, the promised one. . . .

LUCILLUS: Do you think he has already been born?

CARTAPHILUS: I would not know. . . .

LUCILLUS: I think he has—he who is to rule the world and subdue all peoples under his scepter. . . .

CARTAPHILUS: Who could that be?

LUCILLUS: Caesar Augustus!

CARTAPHILUS: Is he of Abraham's seed or of David's house? No! He is not! Has he come with peace as Isaiah prophesied when he said: "His kingdom shall be great, and of peace there shall be no end! . . ."—Indeed, Caesar Augustus is no man of peace. . . .

LUCILLUS: Farewell, you child of Israel. . . . You are now a Roman subject, and you have to be satisfied with the salvation Rome can give you. It's the only salvation there is!

(*He leaves.*)

....

(*Cartaphilus says a silent prayer.*)

....

(*Joseph and Mary pass by with the infant Jesus.*)

End of Scene III

PART II

Scene IV

Before the Roman governor, Pontius Pilate

PILATE: You say then that during my absence Herod the Tetrarch has had a Hebrew named John put to death, and that it has caused much disquiet. What do you know of this matter?

PORCIA: I only know what I have heard in the city. Herod had divorced his wife and married his sister-in-law. When this John, who was a prophet, reproached Herod for his culpable act, the Tetrarch had the Baptist—as he was also called—thrown into prison, and only recently he had him beheaded.

PILATE: The Baptist? Is this the same man who is being spoken of by everyone and who goes under the name of Joshua, or Jesse, or. . . .

PORCIA: You mean Jesus?

PILATE: Yes—the Nazarene, the Galilean . . . or whatever they call him. Is he not the same man?

PORCIA: No, they are two different men. And John is dead now. . . .

PILATE: Strange! But this Jesus baptizes also, heals the sick, and brings back to life the dead, does he not?

PORCIA: They are often mistaken for each other; but they are two different men—or were, I should say.

PILATE: Will you summon the gatekeeper Cartaphilus —he generally is well informed as to what takes place in the city. . . .

PORCIA: I will. But just now we have one of the disciples of the Galilean down in the kitchen. . . . He sometimes brings us fish. . . .

PILATE: Let them both come in. I must put an end to this spectacle.   (*Porcia leaves.*)

....

(*Pilate wanders about; he is uneasy.*)
(*Cartaphilus enters.*)

PILATE: Did you bring the fisherman with you?

CARTAPHILUS: He waits outside.

PILATE: What is his name?

CARTAPHILUS: Simon, commonly called Peter.

PILATE: An Israelite?

CARTAPHILUS: An Israelite.

PILATE: Have you seen the man whom they call Jesus?

CARTAPHILUS: No—he is not to be seen by everyone.

PILATE: What do you mean—that he appears only to some?

CARTAPHILUS: Many speak of him—yet only a few get a glimpse of him. He avoids large gatherings and often takes refuge in the wilderness and the lonely desert.

PILATE: Call the fisherman!   (*Cartaphilus goes out.*)

....

(*Pilate moves about restlessly.*)

....

(*Simon Peter enters.*)

PILATE: Your name is Simon, and you sell fish. . . .

SIMON: Yes, Sire.

PILATE: You knew the man called John who has just been beheaded, did you not?

SIMON: I knew him.

PILATE: Who was he? Where was he born?

SIMON: He was born in the land of Judah, the son of the high priest Zacharias and his wife Elisabeth; but he was born through divine power, for his parents were beyond the age of giving birth.

PILATE: What do you mean by divine power?—Were these two not his rightful parents?

SIMON: Sire, we do not speak the same language and do not serve the same gods. . . . Why do you question me?

PILATE: How dare you put questions to me, you worm? Answer me—tell me more about John's birth and what happened when he was born.

SIMON: The priest Zacharias was filled with the Holy Ghost when he saw the child being born, and he prophesied: "Praised be the Lord, the God of Israel, for He has visited His people and set them free. And you, child," he said to John, "you shall be called the Prophet of the Omnipotent One."

PILATE: Do you mean to imply that John was the Messiah?

SIMON: No—he was the precursor.

PILATE: Of whom?

SIMON: Of Jesus.

PILATE: Then they are two?—Under what special circumstances was Jesus born? Do you know?

SIMON: He, too, was born through divine power, and his birth was prophesied.

PILATE: And you believe he is the Messiah?

SIMON: He is the Messiah.

PILATE: He is to liberate you from the Romans?

SIMON: He shall set us free from the dominions of Sin—and with us, all men. . . .

PILATE: Sin? What is Sin?

SIMON: Evilness.

PILATE: What is evilness—what is goodness? Be on your way, you stupid fool, and go and look after your nets. . . .

End of Scene IV

Scene V

The fore-court of the Temple

PILATE: Speak, Herod! Your heart is full, and your mind is uneasy.

HEROD: Yes—I had this John beheaded and thought that would be the end of it. . . . But now he has come back!

PILATE: Jesus is not the same man—he is a different one.

HEROD: So you think! But I believe he is John who has come back to life. . . .

PILATE: The people once thought that John was their Messiah; but John spoke of the coming of Jesus.

HEROD: Is it not possible to get a glance at this man of whom everyone speaks?

PILATE: I do not think it very easy, for one moment he is here, and the next somewhere else.

HEROD: No doubt he is a magician or a sorcerer—like so many in these days.

PILATE: Yes—but the people nevertheless seem to believe that he is the promised one who has come to save them.

HEROD: Strange! But he is said to have been born in Bethlehem during the last years of Caesar Augustus' reign, when my father, Herod the Great, was disturbed by the rumor that a king of the Jews had just been given birth. That is why he had all male infants who were born in Bethlehem at that time, put to death. Is it possible that this one could have escaped?

PILATE: They say that he was brought up in Heliopolis in Egypt.

HEROD: That is already thirty years ago—and only now is he beginning to be heard of. . . .

PILATE: Let us ask the High Priest . . . he should be able to tell us.

HEROD: I hear a tumult from near the temple!

PILATE: I can imagine what has started it.

HEROD: Is it because they are putting up the statue of the Emperor?

PILATE: Yes, that's the cause of it! Our gracious Tiberius is living like a madman on Capri, accepts beatings from his nephew Caligula—if he can be called nephew, since the sons are married to their mothers; but this does not prevent the Emperor from ordering his own deification.

HEROD: Antiochus Epiphanes had the god Zeus placed in the holiest of holies of the Jews. But Zeus, I must say, was a god, a real god!—If they put up a likeness of that creature Tiberius, there will be a revolution!

PILATE: Well, what can we do about it?—Here comes Caiphas. . . .   (*Caiphas enters.*)

HEROD: What is all this noise from the temple?

CAIPHAS: It is the Galilean who is again leading the people astray! Now he is indulging in violence and is driving the money changers from the temple.

HEROD: Then let us take a look at him while he is there!

CAIPHAS: He is already gone.

PILATE: Tell us, High Priest, what is so unusual about this man? Do you think that he is the Messiah who has been promised you?

CAIPHAS: How could I think that? The son of a poor carpenter—who is sick in the head? Away with that thought!

PILATE: What is it he is teaching?

CAIPHAS: He teaches the people disobedience to our laws; he breaks the Sabbath; he refuses to keep the fast days; he disrupts family bonds and exhorts our youth to abandon father and mother for his sake; he gives himself out to be the son of Jehovah. . . .

PILATE: Have you any witnesses?

CAIPHAS: Yes—but they contradict one another. . . .

HEROD: Get better witnesses!

PILATE: You know, High Priest, that the Emperor— through a decision of the Senate—has been deified, and that his image is about to be placed in the temple.

CAIPHAS: We exist through the grace of our Emperor —but if such an abomination is put into effect, we shall all seek death—as our Maccabees once did.

PILATE: Then go to your death!

CAIPHAS: I shall summon the High Council and tell them the will of the Emperor.

PILATE: One thing more! You shall—before the Passover—bring that Galilean before me! It is my wish to see him!

CAIPHAS: I shall do that!

PILATE: Go in peace!   (*Caiphas leaves.*)

....

PILATE: They are a hard people! You, too, are of Israel, are you not, Herod?

HEROD: Not of Jacob's house, but of Esau's. I am an Edomite, and my mother was a Samaritan, one of a despised tribe. Jacob stole his birthright from Esau; that is why I do not care for Jacob and the twelve tribes.

PILATE: I wish I had never seen this land! Nothing good will ever come out of it. . . .

End of Scene V

Scene VI

Before the Great Sanhedrin

CAIPHAS: Since we cannot escape the abomination of having the Emperor's image placed in the Holiest of Holies, and since people are bound to die in the uprising, I think it better that we now observe our sacrifice to the Lord and that one man die for all the people!

ANNAS: An extraordinary sacrifice as atonement is what we need, and since the Passover is approaching, let us offer up the Galilean.

CAIPHAS: But the offering must be a clean one, a pure one, in order to please the Lord! Iscariot, is the Galilean that?

JUDAS: Pure and innocent as a lamb!

CAIPHAS: Then may he take the sins of Israel upon himself that we may be saved through his blood! . . . Iscariot will hand him over to us!—(*To Judas Iscariot.*) You have set your price, have you not?

JUDAS: Thirty pieces of silver!

CAIPHAS (*Counts out the money*): There you have them!—Now go! (*Judas leaves.*)

....

CAIPHAS: Annas, has not the prophet Zachariah written: "And so they weighed for me my price: thirty pieces of silver"?

ANNAS: So he wrote, yes—and he added: "And I took the thirty pieces of silver and cast them to the potter in the house of the Lord."

CAIPHAS: Let the other disciple come in!

....

(John the Evangelist enters.)

CAIPHAS: What witness can you give about your teacher? Has he raised his voice against the law of Moses? Has he?

JOHN: He has fulfilled the law.

CAIPHAS: But which new commandment has he added to our sacred laws?

JOHN: Love one another—love your enemies—bless them who curse you. . . .

CAIPHAS: Have you heard him say that he is the King of the Jews?

JOHN: The Master has said: "My kingdom is not of this world."

CAIPHAS: Has he exhorted the children to rise up against their parents?

JOHN: The Master has said: "He who loves his father and mother more than he loves God, is not worthy of me."

CAIPHAS: Has he said that people have the right to neglect their civil duties? Has he?

JOHN: The Master has said: "Seek ye first the kingdom of God and His righteousness; then all these other things shall be added unto you."

CAIPHAS: Has he told the laborer to abandon his task?

JOHN: The Master has said: "Come unto me, all ye that labor and are heavy laden, and I will give you rest."

CAIPHAS: Has he said that he will conquer the whole world?

JOHN: The Master has said: "In the world you shall have tribulation, but be of good cheer: I have overcome the world. "

....

ANNAS: Of all that I have heard or perceived, this man has not answered a single one of your questions.

JOHN: Because the Master answers in truth and spirit, but you scribes and Pharisees judge things after the flesh and not the Spirit. Between us is a sword—we are not children of the same Spirit.

CAIPHAS: I do not understand a word of what he says.

JOHN: He has sent me to preach the gospel to the poor; to heal the brokenhearted; to preach deliverance to the captives; to give sight to the blind; and to set at liberty them that are bruised.

ANNAS: What you have spoken in ignorance, young man, can do neither you nor your Master any good.

JOHN: Woe to you when human beings praise you. And he who turns away from evil, he will be the prey of every man!

CAIPHAS: Go!   (*John leaves.*)

....

CAIPHAS: This new kind of wisdom is to me sheer madness.

ANNAS: Such speech is to me like a strange language. A kingdom not of this world! What nonsense is this!

CAIPHAS: He is indeed no Messiah! And he must die his death!

ANNAS (*Together with the members of the Sanhedrin*): Amen!

End of Scene VI

Scene VII

A street in Jerusalem

LUCILLUS: What are they waiting for? They are all waiting—but nobody knows for what.

CARTAPHILUS: Israel is waiting for the fulfillment of the promise and for the restoring of their kingdom. What are the Romans waiting for?

LUCILLUS: The Romans are waiting for the fall of their empire. While patricians and plebeians existed—competing with each other and bending their every effort in the interest of the State—just so long did the State endure. . . . But now they are all plebeians—the emperor's pawns—and that is why the State is crumbling.

CARTAPHILUS: Israel shall build upon Rome.

LUCILLUS: Has the Galilean said so?

CARTAPHILUS: Now *you* speak of him—two persons cannot meet anywhere without speaking of him. . . . Who is he? He himself says he is the son of God, the Messiah, the Saviour of the World. . . .

LUCILLUS: He eats and drinks with the rabble and the people at the customs—so he must be a human being.

CARTAPHILUS: A human being—and more than a human being.—Where are you bound for?

LUCILLUS: I am going to the stadium to watch the gladiators. And you?

CARTAPHILUS: I am going to prepare the paschal lamb for my family.   (*They both leave.*)

PETER (*Enters with John*): Jesus said: "Go into the city, and when you meet a man bearing a pitcher of water, ask him where the Master will eat passover with his disciples. And he will show you the chamber."—We have gone street up and street down, and yet have not met the man. . . . What are we to think?

JOHN: Peter, be steadfast in your hope. . . .

PETER: In my hope? Hope in what? Did not the Master say that he was to be sacrificed this very Passover? What have we then to hope for?

JOHN: That he shall be near us eternally, forevermore.

PETER: And we are to reign with him and sit in judgment on the twelve tribes of Israel?

JOHN: With your impatience and your ignorance, you will betray your Master. . . .

PETER: I? Even if all the others should deny and betray him, I shall not!

....

JUDAS   (*Enters*):   What are you seeking?

PETER: The chamber where the Master is to eat passover with us.

JUDAS: Oh, oh!

JOHN: You will be with us, will you not?

JUDAS: Certainly, yes. . . .

JOHN: You have come from the governor's—from Pilate?

JUDAS: Yes. They have imprisoned a murderer.

JOHN: A revolutionary? And you were a witness?

JUDAS: I witnessed.

JOHN: You are eager to witness, are you not?

JUDAS: When it comes to murderers and revolutionaries, yes. I like law and order.

JOHN: The murderer's name was Barabbas, was it not?

JUDAS: How did you know?

JOHN: The whole community knows it!

....

(*Zaccheus the customs official enters.*)

ZACCHEUS: Is the Master here?

PETER: No! What is it you want? Who are you?

ZACCHEUS: I am Zaccheus, the customs official—the petty sinner in the fig tree, whom the Master came to visit.

JUDAS: But you are not one of his disciples. . . .

ZACCHEUS: The humblest one among them—though not one of the twelve.

JUDAS: What do you want of the Master?

ZACCHEUS: I wish to tell him that one of the twelve is betraying him!

JUDAS: Who?

ZACCHEUS: That I will tell him myself.

....

(*The Man with the Pitcher of Water enters.*)

JOHN   (*Turns to him*): The Master wishes me to ask you: "Where is the chamber where I am to eat supper with my disciples?"

THE MAN: There—in there is the chamber—enter!

JOHN: Simon Peter, do you believe now?

PETER: I believe!   (*They enter the house.*)

End of Scene VII

Scene VIII

At Gethsemane

JACOB: What is the Master doing?

PETER: He is praying. I can hear him speak: "Then remove this cup from me; yet, let not my will be done but Yours!"

JOHN: You can see the agony he is suffering—his sweat is as great drops of blood.

PETER: Why does he not ask his Father for a legion of angels to defend him?

JOHN: Because his mission on this earth has to be fulfilled. . . .

JACOB: What mission.

JOHN: The act of atonement!

PETER: Will that bring peace on earth, then?

JOHN: Yes—it will!

PETER: Do you understand how?

JOHN: I do not understand—but I believe! The Master has said so!

JACOB: Arise and let us leave, for he who is to betray him is come.

....

JUDAS (*Enters. He is accompanied by a detachment of soldiers*): Is the Master here?

PETER: He is inside. . . .

End of Scene VIII

Scene IX

At Pilate's

PILATE: I have questioned the Galilean, and I can find no cause for holding him.

CAIPHAS: He is inciting the people to rebellion.

PILATE: No—it is Barabass who is stirring up the people.

CAIPHAS: He says he is the King of the Jews.

PILATE: But he also says that his kingdom is not of this world!

CAIPHAS: Then let the people judge!

PILATE: Very well! It is the Feast of the Passover, and one prisoner shall be set free. . . . Let the people be the judge between Jesus and Barabbas! . . . The voice of the people is the voice of God—and they cannot but set free their benefactor!

CAIPHAS: We are agreed: May the people judge!

PILATE (*Goes to the window and speaks to the multitude outside*): Shall I set free Jesus or Barabbas? . . . Whom shall I set free: Jesus or Barabbas?

THE PEOPLE (*Outside*): Set free Barabbas!

PILATE: Barabbas!—Forever Barabbas! O people, O land. . . . . O land!—What, then, do you wish me to do with Jesus, your benefactor, your king, your Saviour?

THE PEOPLE: Let him be crucified! Crucify him!

PILATE: I wash my hands of this, I am innocent of the blood of this righteous man!

THE PEOPLE: Crucify him! Crucify! Let his blood be on us and on our children!

PILATE: So be it!

End of Scene IX

Scene X

Golgotha

Only the shadows of the three crosses can be seen against a white cliff of limestone.

THE SOLDIER: Truly this man was a righteous man and the son of God!

JOHN   (*To Mary*): It is fulfilled!

End of Scene X

PART III

Scene XI

The Temple of Jupiter Latiaris in Rome, showing the statue of Caligula as Jupiter

LUCILLUS: Here we meet again, Hebrew.

CARTAPHILUS: The Romans we meet everywhere; they are at home everywhere—but are nowhere at home.

LUCILLUS: Do you see now that the Romans have inherited the promise to possess the earth?

CARTAPHILUS: For how long?

LUCILLUS: As long as the cross stands upright.

CARTAPHILUS: Are you . . . ?

LUCILLUS: I am a Christian—yes!

CARTAPHILUS: What is a Christian?

LUCILLUS: A Christian is. . . I can not say it—for it must not be spoken—just as *your* God's name must not be spoken.

CARTAPHILUS: Do you believe he was the son of God?

LUCILLUS: I believe!

CARTAPHILUS: Can you give me proof of that?

LUCILLUS: No—not to you.

CARTAPHILUS: Was he the son of Jehovah?

LUCILLUS: The son of the Father—and the Saviour of the World!

CARTAPHILUS: Empty words!

LUCILLUS: To you, madness—yes; to us the highest in wisdom.

CARTAPHILUS: Whose temple is this?

LUCILLUS: It is the temple of the Beast—the temple of

Caligula, emperor, murderer, blood revenger, madman—who now rules the whole of the visible world!

CARTAPHILUS: Where is the *invisible* world?

LUCILLUS: All about us! Socrates and Plato divined it —Christ saw it and showed us the way.

CARTAPHILUS: Show it to me!

LUCILLUS: Can you see the wind? No—but you can see the ship move from the force of the wind. The wind is invisible—yet you would not deny its existence, would you?

CARTAPHILUS: Where do you live?

LUCILLUS: Beneath Rome . . . underneath here—down in the caves and catacombs in the rock. . . . But one day we shall come up and see the light of day—and then Rome shall rule the world for a second time!

CARTAPHILUS: You live underneath here—inside the earth?

LUCILLUS: There is where we Christians dwell—there is where we lie like seed in the earth and keep growing. . . .

CARTAPHILUS: Is it not there that the dead are buried?

LUCILLUS: Yes—we are buried with Christ, and are awaiting the day of resurrection.

CARTAPHILUS: Have you a temple down there?

LUCILLUS: We hold our services down there, and tonight we celebrate the birth of Jesus.

CARTAPHILUS (*Gives a start*): Someone is coming!

LUCILLUS (*Opens a trapdoor in the floor; from below is heard the singing of the Christians*):

And the city needs neither sun nor moon,
for the glory of God enlightens it,
and the Lamb is our light. . . .

CARTAPHILUS: Who is the lamb?

LUCILLUS: Jesus Christ, the Saviour of the World.

CARTAPHILUS: Would you say that the world has been saved while that madman Caligula is acting as God?

LUCILLUS: The world will be saved if we are unswerving in our hope!

CARTAPHILUS: You have purloined the promise that was given Israel.

LUCILLUS: We have inherited the promise given to Israel, for Christ was of Israel's Judah!

CARTAPHILUS (*Starts to leave*): Someone is coming!

LUCILLUS: Farewell, then! We will meet again, for the earth is ours.

CARTAPHILUS: Farewell! (*He goes.*)

(*Lucillus descends through the trapdoor which is left open.*)

....

CALIGULA (*Enters, dressed as Jupiter. Frightened, he steals alongside the walls*): Is the priest here?—Priest!

(*The Priest enters.*)

CALIGULA: Priest, dear priest, I am so frightened. . . . I cannot sleep nights. . . .

THE PRIEST (*Kneels before Caligula*): Jupiter, Optimus Maximus, put fear into your enemies!

CALIGULA: That is why I am afraid—because I have enemies!—Do you believe that I am God?

THE PRIEST: Of course you are God! Let your lightning strike and your thunder crash, and your enemies will flee!

CALIGULA: Is everything in order and ready?

THE PRIEST: When I pull the cord, the thunder will start. . . . Seat yourself on your throne!

CALIGULA (*Seats himself on the throne*): Start the thunder!

(*The Priest pulls a cord and there is a crash of thunder.*)

CALIGULA (*Laughs*): Now I shall frighten them! Ha ha!—Priest, offer up a sacrifice to me that I may feel my power!

(*The Priest lights a fire on the altar.*)

CALIGULA: It smells nice! Now I am mightier than anyone on earth and in heaven! I sit in judgment over all that is living and dead— I can cast them away in the Tartarus or I can elevate them to the Elysium! Just think of the power that is mine! I can calm the waves of the sea and tame the storm—I rule the orbits of the planets—and it was I who created chaos! Hahah! And the human race is crawling at my feet, from the primeval forests of Britannia to the sources of the Nile! I have elevated my stallion Incitatus and made him a priest and a Roman consul—and the Romans have applauded his promotion!—Priest! Adore me!—Or are you forgetting who I am?—No—it is I who must set a good example—it is I who must adore myself!—in my own image!

(*He kneels before his own statue.*)

Caius Caesar Caligula, I adore you, Lord of the World, as I adore myself! Jupiter Latiaris Caligula. . . .

THE PRIEST: Someone is coming!

CALIGULA: Then let him die!

THE PRIEST: It is Cassius Chaerea.

CALIGULA: Let the thunder roar!

THE PRIEST (*Trying in vain to pull the cord*): The cord has snapped. . . .

....

CHAEREA (*Enters*): Caius Caesar, your wife has been murdered. . . .

CALIGULA: Good riddance!

CHAEREA: Your only child has been crushed against a wall!

CALIGULA: That is really comic!

CHAEREA: And now you shall die!

CALIGULA: I can never die! I am immortal!

CHAEREA: I shall be waiting for you outside. This is not the place for it!   (*He goes out.*)

CALIGULA: Crawl, you insect—my foot is too noble for vermin like you!

....

THE PRIEST: Caius Caesar, now it is lightning!
CALIGULA: It is only I doing it! What are you afraid of?
THE PRIEST: No—it is thundering—it is a real thunderstorm!   (*One hears the thunder.*)
CALIGULA: Who has the audacity to touch my thunder?
THE PRIEST: It is Jupiter himself! Jupiter tonans!
CALIGULA: Which Jupiter?
THE PRIEST: The God of the heavens!   (*It thunders.*)
THE PRIEST: Mercy!   (*The Priest flees.*)
CALIGULA: Stay, priest! Stay! I am frightened!
   (*He treads his way falteringly alongside the walls.*)
I am frightened! I am frightened!—And I hear things— I hear voices from underneath—something about a lamb and —and a little child. . . . I am so frightened—so frightened. . . .
                           (*He crawls under the throne.*)
. . . and I cannot sleep nights—I ought to go and take a bath. . . . Oh, now it is thundering again—if it would only stop thundering. . . .

....

CHAEREA   (*Enters*): Are you coming, you dog—or do I have to put you to death in here?
CALIGULA: Chaerea, do not kill me! I shall kiss your foot, if you will only let me live!
CHAEREA: Then kiss it while I am trampling you to death, you rotten beast!
                  (*He tramples Caligula to death, then leaves.*)

....

(*From below in the catacombs can be heard:*)
Glory to God in the highest—
on earth peace—
And good will toward men!

End of Scene XI

Scene XII

In the Palace of Emperor Claudius in Rome

Claudius is playing dice with Caius Silius.

CLAUDIUS: Pay attention to the game.
SILIUS: I do.
CLAUDIUS: No, your thoughts are elsewhere. . . .
Where were you last night?
SILIUS: I was in Suburra.
CLAUDIUS: You must not go to Suburra. You must
stay here with me. I am afraid to be alone.
SILIUS: When was a Claudius afraid?
CLAUDIUS: When we became the masters of the
world. We now have Britannia and Germania.—Pay atten-
tion to the game!
SILIUS: What stakes are we playing for?
CLAUDIUS: You are playing for your life!
SILIUS: And you!
CLAUDIUS: For the same stakes: your life!
SILIUS: And if you lose?
CLAUDIUS: Then *you* lose your life!

....

(*Narcissus enters.*)

CLAUDIUS: Give me the writing materials, Narcissus!
. . . Against snake bite one uses the sap of the yew tree. . . .
SILIUS: And against the poisonous herb Cienta—what?
CLAUDIUS: Cienta? There is no antidote for that!—
Pay attention to the game, or I shall lose my temper!
SILIUS: Could you lose your temper?

CLAUDIUS: No—I have not enough strength for that. . . . I was merely boasting. . . .

....

MESSALINA (*Enters*): Why is Silius sitting here playing games? He was to have gone with me to the amphitheater.

CLAUDIUS: Because I want him to!

MESSALINA: What right have you to monopolize him, you wretch?

CLAUDIUS: He is my slave! All are slaves of the Ruler of the World. That is why Rome is more democratic than it has ever been! All are the same—before me and God!

MESSALINA: He may be your slave—but he is my husband!

CLAUDIUS: Your husband? I am married to you, am I not?

MESSALINA: Well, what difference does that make?

CLAUDIUS: Do you go and get married without asking my permission?

MESSALINA: Y-e-s!

CLAUDIUS: I must say, you are an amusing woman, Messalina. . . . And I forgive you.—Go then, my children, and enjoy yourselves. . . . Narcissus will play with me.

MESSALINA: Come, Silius!

(*Messalina and Silius leave.*)

....

CLAUDIUS: Narcissus, follow them! Take along Locusta—and give them the cup with the sleeping potion—then I can take Agrippina! —   (*He falls asleep.*)

(*Narcissus gets up.*)

....

LUCILLUS (*Enters*): Is he asleep?

NARCISSUS: No—he is merely sleepy.

LUCILLUS: If this is the Ruler of the World—then what must the world be like? This is the second one of the bestial creatures! Is the lamb predestined to perish, then?

NARCISSUS: No! The lamb will conquer the beast!

End of Scene XII

Scene XIII

At the Court of Emperor Nero in Rome

LUCILLUS: Now we have our third beast among us!
Nero—the worthy son of Agrippina—poisons his stepbrother
Britannicus, murders his own mother, brutally kicks his wife
to death—and now he is marrying a gladiator!—Can this be
the end of the world?

PALLAS: And that is not all! He makes counterfeit
money, plunders the temples, and is now contemplating
putting Rome on fire. He has made a journey to Greece in
the interest of art, has been a charioteer, but upset the char-
iot and yet demanded all the prizes!—This is how deep Hellas has sunk—and Rome!— Claudius—beast though he was
—was an angel in comparison with *this* beast who has now
been accepted as one of the gods!—Married in public—in a
religious ceremony—to a gladiator!

LUCILLUS: He is coming!

PALLAS: Then my life is at an end!—Brother—we shall
meet again—pray for me—and give me your brotherly kiss!

LUCILLUS: The Lord shall redeem you of all evil and
save you for his heavenly kingdom! The perishable must
clothe itself with the imperishable, and the mortal must
take on the garb of immortality.

....

NERO (*Enters*): Pallas! Rome is burning!

(*Pallas is silent.*)

NERO: Are you deaf?   (*Pallas remains silent.*)

NERO: Have you no tongue?

(*Pallas is still silent.*)

NERO: Rome is burning, and they are saying that I
put it on fire! I did not—but they think it would be quite

like me to have done it! Do you hear the yelling and screaming? . . . Pallas—go out in the city and spread the word that the Christians put Rome on fire!

PALLAS: I will not!

NERO: Did I hear aright? Don't you know that the Christians are sorcerers and that they live like rats down in the catacombs—that the whole city of Rome is resting upon Christians? . . . I had thought of diverting the Tiber and drowning them, or bursting open the walls of the sewers and inundating the catacombs with excrements and offal. . . . I hate them, for they are undermining the temples of our gods so that we get neither oracle nor any help. . . . I met one of those demons once, and that night I could not get any sleep. . . . Their Sibylline books have presaged the ruin of Rome—but they do not call it Rome; they call it Babel . . . . Look—now the fire has spread to the Capitolium. . . . Pallas—go out into the city and raise the cry that the Christians are to blame. . . . Go!

PALLAS: I will not stoop to lies!

NERO: This time I heard aright!—You refuse to go into the city, do you? Well, then you will take this passageway here—you know where it leads—and you will face my little feline pets! . . .

(*He opens an iron gate and pushes Pallas inside.*)

PALLAS: Lucillus! I exhort you to be steadfast—and strong—and fearless! . . .

LUCILLUS: I know that my redeemer lives and that he shall resurrect me from the dust of death when the world is at an end.

NERO: What manner of speech is that you are using? —Lucillus, go out into the city and spread the word that the Christians have set Rome on fire!

LUCILLUS: No. . . . I am a Christian.

NERO: Now I am frightened! What is a Christian?

LUCILLUS: For God so loved the world that He gave His only begotten Son that whosoever believes in Him shall not perish but have everlasting life.

NERO: You mean that you will live forever? That I have not the power to kill you?

LUCILLUS: You have no power to take my life, unless the power be given you from above. . . . You may destroy my body, but only to liberate my soul, to give it peace and bliss in the eternal life. . . .

NERO: He has no fear of death!—Narcissus! Come here and bring some fire!—I shall set fire to your garments, Lucillus—then we shall see whether you can burn or not! I shall fire your hair, beard, your nails; but first I shall drench you with oil and naphtha; I shall cover you with tar and sulphur—then we shall see if you will live an eternal life! . . . Narcissus! . . .

....

NARCISSUS   (*Enters*): Sire, there is rebellion in the city! Flee!

NERO: I—flee. . . ?—Set fire to the city!—Burn it down!

NARCISSUS: Hispania has revolted and Galba has been proclaimed emperor!

NERO: Galba! Let us flee! But where—where?

NARCISSUS: Through the catacombs, out to the Campagna di Roma!

NERO: The catacombs?—No—there is where the Christians live, and they would kill me!

LUCILLUS: They kill no one!

NERO: Not even their enemies?

LUCILLUS: They pray for their enemies. . . .

NERO: Then they must be crazy—stark crazy!—Very well—let us flee, then, Narcissus! . . .

End of Scene XIII

Scene XIV

In the Catacombs

Lucillus, Erastus, and Alexander are discovered at the rise of the curtain.

GAIUS (*Enters*): Christ is risen!

LUCILLUS (*and the others*): Glory be to God!

GAIUS: Our friend Peter is dead!

ALL: Dead?

GAIUS: He has been crucified—he, the Lord's disciple —our firm protection—the pillar of our congregation. . . .

ERASTUS: The beast has torn asunder the lamb! . . .

ALEXANDER: Lord, You who are the truth, and holy, how long before You shall sit in judgment and avenge our blood and visit Your revenge upon those who dwell on earth? . . .

GAIUS: Away with such evil talk!—"Father, forgive them, for they know not what they do!"

....

(*Timothy enters.*)

ALEXANDER: Here comes that Germanic man. . . .

GAIUS: Here we are neither Jew nor Greek, nor Barbarian, nor Scythian . . . we are neither servants nor are we free . . . we are all brothers in Christ!—Welcome, brother!

TIMOTHY: Our lives are in danger—the mob is killing our brethren!

GAIUS: Then may we die!—Christ rose, did he not?.

TIMOTHY: Our friend Peter has been crucified!

GAIUS: But he shall rise again and sit on a throne of glory and judge all the tribes of the world.

ALEXANDER: After he is dead?

GAIUS: Yes—through those who come after him!—This was the promise he received of the Messiah: that upon him, Peter, our church was to be built.

LUCILLUS: Someone is coming in the passageway. . . .

GAIUS: Is it one of our brethren?

LUCILLUS: No—he does not kneel before the cross. . . .

GAIUS: If it be our turn to die—so be it!

....

(*Nero enters. His garments are torn, and he holds a handkerchief before his face*):

LUCILLUS: It is Nero!

ALL: The bestial brute!

....

NERO (*Falls on his knees*): Do not kill me! I have lost my way!—I am a poor stonecutter. . . . Show me which way to take—whether the one to the right or the left. . . .

LUCILLUS: Where do you wish to go, you poor fellow?

NERO: Out to the Campagna. . . .

LUCILLUS: Do you recognize me?

NERO: Lucillus!

LUCILLUS: Whom you wanted to put to death by fire! —Yes—it is I!

NERO: Mercy! Do not kill me!

LUCILLUS: Arise, Caesar. Your life is in God's hand— and before Him all mankind shall bend the knee. . . .

NERO: Have mercy on me! Will you not help me to find the way out?

LUCILLUS: I shall provide you with a guide. . . .

NERO: There is no need for that! Just tell me whether to go to the right or the left—then I can find the way myself!

LUCILLUS: Keep to the left!

NERO: But if you are lying to me!

LUCILLUS: That is something I can not do—and that, you see, is the difference between you and me!

NERO: Why should you not tell a lie? That is what I would do!

LUCILLUS: Keep to the left!

NERO   (*As he goes, he turns and spits*): Faugh, you slaves!—Now I can take care of myself!

LUCILLUS: There you saw the wild beast!

End of Scene XIV

Scene XV

In front of Phaon's country home

A pond. A bench of reed.
It is thundering.

NERO   (*He is pounding on the entrance door*): Open, Phaon!

PHAON   (*Opens the door*): Is it you, Sire?

NERO: Not so loud—I am being followed! Let me in!

PHAON: No—not in here—there is a soldier inside!

NERO: Then hide me somewhere! I am afraid of the thunder!

PHAON: Hide among the reeds, Caesar!

NERO: No—the water is too cold, and I would sink down in the mire! Then I would rather take Locusta's poison!

PHAON: That, I believe, would be the best thing you could do—else the Senate judgment would be executed!

NERO: What judgment?

PHAON: Do you not know?

NERO: Have I been condemned?

PHAON: Yes, you are condemned to die!—Hide among the rushes! A soldier is coming this way!

NERO   (*Searching for something in his garments*): Woe, I have lost the poison potion! I cannot die!

"O say, can any mortal on this earth find happiness?
Alas, the loftiest is overthrown and brought to ruin!"

PHAON: Be silent! They are coming!

....

(*Two Soldiers enter.*)

FIRST SOLDIER: Is the matricide here?

PHAON: Whom do you mean?

SECOND SOLDIER: Nero—he has murdered his mother! The Senate has condemned him to be flogged to death!

PHAON: He is not here!   (*The Soldiers disappear.*)

....

NERO: How lucky for humanity that there is still a man who dares to lie! . . . Phaon, help me—give me a dagger —give me a knife. . . .

"Where shall I go—where stay? . . . No word describes
    the pain I feel!—
If I were only dead!
My mother bore me to a sorry fate. . .
How lucky are the dead!—They may be envied. . . ."

Kill me, Phaon—I have not the courage to kill myself!

PHAON: Here is the dagger, Caesar—I cannot be a murderer.

NERO: Why can you not?

PHAON: I cannot!

NERO: Then I shall kill myself!—To be flogged to death—never!—Look at me! This is how a hero dies—the greatest of the sons of Rome—the noblest of all hearts! Humanity, you shall feel my loss and grieve!

PHAON: Hasten, Caesar! I see more soldiers coming here!

NERO: Your dagger is not sharp enough—it fails to bite!

PHAON: Aim at the heart, Caesar!

NERO (*Starts to sob*): No—I cannot! How could I do away with a human life such as mine!

PHAON: Then you will be flogged to death!

NERO: Could they really have the heart to flog me!— See—my blood is floating in the pond, and the ravens are gathering to weep tears. . . . They feel pity for Nero! . . .

....

(*The Slave enters.*)

NERO: Slave, do you know your master?

THE SLAVE: Yes, Caesar.

NERO: Help me to get out of this life. . . . I am dying!

THE SLAVE: If you are dying, I shall help you. . . .

(*He stabs Nero, who falls to the ground.*)

NERO: The last one of Caesar Augustus' dynasty—the last one of the Romans is dead! Who shall now inherit the throne?

PHAON: The Galilean!

C U R T A I N